Rise and Fall of a Multi-Million Dollar Brand

I did it my way…

Rise and Fall of a Multi-Million Dollar Brand

I did it my way…

Stacey M King

Banaban Vision Publication
GOLD COAST, AUSTRALIA

Rise and Fall of a Multi-Million Dollar Brand – I did it my way ...
Copyright © 2020 by Stacey M King

All rights reserved. No part of this book may be reproduced in any form or by any electronic or mechanical means, including information storage and retrieval system, without permission in writing from the author. The only exception is by a reviewer who may quote short excerpts in a review.

ISBN: 978-0-6485462-8-3   Paperback
       978-0-6451491-1-1   eBook

 A catalogue record for this book is available from the National Library of Australia

Cataloguing in Publication Data
Author: Stacey M King
Title: Rise and Fall of a Multi-Million Dollar Brand - I did it my way ...
Published: Gold Coast, Banaban Vision Publications, 2021.
Subjects: Biography, Business

While all the characters in this book are based on real characters, various names have been altered to protect the privacy of those involved. All the events expressed in this book are solely from the author's viewpoint.

Edited: Ian Mathieson *iEdit*

Front cover image: Stacey M King
All photographs: Stacey M King unless otherwise credited.

Published: Banaban Vision Publications 2020
PO Box 1116, Paradise Point. Qld. 4216. Australia
www.banabanvision.com

DEDICATION

To my mother, who always insisted that "the best is yet to be". She was my greatest supporter, my ally and my confidant.

I am blessed to have had strong women in my life who have been wonderful role models; embedding their strength, determination and pioneering spirit in my DNA.

To my three amazing children who grew up with me, always "chasing rainbows".

I know it was not always easy, but the most important gift in life is our spirit and belief that dreams can come true.

To Ken, my hero, my champion, my warrior; no one will ever know the depth of understanding and strength we shared.

CONTENTS

Dedication v
Photographs x
Introduction 1
The Banaban Cause 5
My Driving Force 9
    I Wish I was Clever? 12
    A "Light Bulb" Moment 14
    Reality Check - Poverty 22
God's Gift 31
    Returning to a Harrowing Retail World 36
    Turning a Cause into a Mission 39
    Garage of Dreams 43
    Customers Where I Least Expected 47
    The Italian Connection, Swimming with Sharks 49
    A World at My Fingertips 53
Sleepless Nights 61
    Being in Demand 64
    The Curse of Cyclones 68
    Turning a Negative into a Positive 69
Don't Miss the Opportunities 75
    Creating a Brand 80
    Online to Retail to Wholesale to Bulk 85
    Going Global 91
    Online Sales - Shipping from Australia 94
    Setting Up Global Distributors 96
    Full Containers vs Less Container Load 111

- Supply Chain Management/Logistics 114
- Fulfilment Centres/Third Party Logistics (3PL) 115
- Exporting Bulk Shipments 117

The Big Question – China? 121
- Alibaba China 121
- China Market Challenges 124
- The World is Waiting 128

A Dream Investor with No Hidden Agenda 129
- Avoiding Punchups in the Office 135
- Hang on for the Ride 149
- Finally, Mainstream Distribution 153
- We Made It – I think? 156
- Palace of Dreams 159
- The Price of Success 166

Can We Help You Spend Your Hard-Earned Money? ... 173
- What is Debtor Finance 174
- Life Back Home in the Islands 177
- Success Now Our Enemy 183
- Success – a Two-Edged Sword 191
- Who Do You Trust? 200
- When Export Deals Go Wrong 204
- When Suppliers Let You Down 214

Hold on to the Dream 235
- The Vultures are Circling 239
- It's Lonely at the Top 245
- Family Business – the Bane of Investors 247
- The Vultures Have Landed 250
- The Offer 259
- Heading into Battle 262

Welcome to the Cutthroat Corporate World 271
- When is an MOU Not an MOU? 274
- Board Meetings from Hell 278
- When Enough – Is Enough 282

   Broken Promises 288
   Breaking Point 295
The New Vision 299
   What the New Vision Really Meant 301
   Bring on Safe Harbour – Like Hell! 308
   Oh Bill, Oh Bill, Where Art Thou Bill? 313
Gauging Success: What Does It All Mean? 323
   Walking Away with a Smile on My Face 327
Postscript 331
About the Author 337

PHOTOGRAPHS

1. Four generations Stacey's family Banaba 1900s 4
2. Stacey and Ken asked to write Banaba history. 8
3. Stacey in first shop Orchid Ave, Surfers Paradise 20
4. We were so poor, and yet so happy! 24
5. Tribal Pacifica's success selling globally. 30
6. Where it all began. The Garage of Dreams 40
7. A busines started on $4.50 product 56
8. Ken's niece Geness face of Banaban brand 60
9. Creating a strong brand image 74
10. Creating a separate organic range was vital 88
11. The family team outside Factory of Dreams 92
12. Stacey and Ken at FoodEx, Japan 2012 98
13. Banaban Mogolia distributors 112
14. Awarded Alibaba's Top 101 International Seller 120
15. Four Factories of Dreams bulging with stock 136
16. Palace of Dreams. Four factories in one facility. ... 162
17. Brynley visiting coconut farm in Fiji 172
18. Company's export markets and aid projects 180
19. Stacey at her birthday feast in Vanuatu. 206
20. Ken assisting coconut farm with aid. 216
21. Impact of cyclone damage on Fiji farm 224
22. Stacey sailing her yacht every weekend. 234
23. Company's production designed by Ken. 256
24. Stacey's presentation at Alibaba HQ China 270
25. Stacey with Terikano Fiji Coconut conference 284
26. Only one Safe Harbour for Stacey 310
27. After fourteen years our company was gone 318
28. Stacey and Ken at home 2004. 322

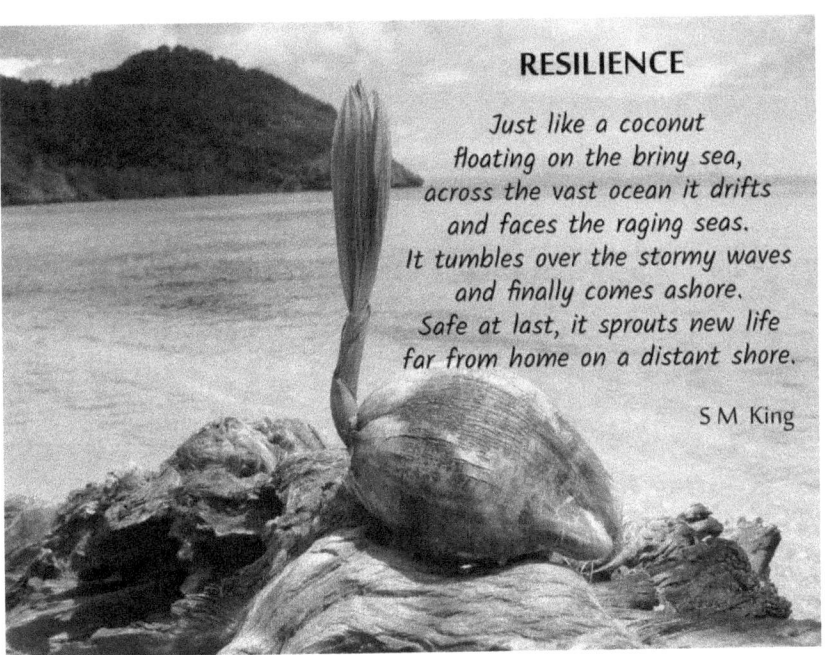

INTRODUCTION

This is my story ... warts and all, of how I did it, my way!

My story is about developing natural products based on centuries of tradition, that empowered hundreds of indigenous people to believe in their own abilities and utilise their inherited skills to enrich their lives. But more importantly, it's about the realisation that western society valued their knowledge.

It is about the amazing people who touched my life: the people in the remotest jungle villages; the corporate executives in the city skyscraper boardrooms; the people from different walks of life and cultures spanning the globe, even as far as the mountains and rolling plains of distant Mongolia. The greatest gift you all gave me was to appreciate the value of our shared humanity.

Just like the cycle of life, the creating of a business and building a brand will change, grow and adapts over time. We only hear about the success stories, but for every success story, there is also a failure. The final phase, or the death of a business, is just as important as how it all began. By sharing my journey, I hope to provide some valuable insight and, above all, support to the younger generations who follow in my footsteps.

Throughout my storyline, a clear pattern emerges — the closing of one door and the opening of the next. How some of the most trivial episodes or experiences can open many opportunities that I never dreamed possible. How to embrace it all, good and bad, and utilise these encounters to enhance my skills and overcome my weaknesses.

I unashamedly write this book from a female perspective. To the amazing, strong and brave women who have done it on their own; sometimes despite their partners, juggling children and the family home, you are and will always be my heroes. To the men who are risking it all; living on the knife's edge, as well as carrying the weight and responsibilities of supporting your loved ones. To all the partners who sometimes feel their marriages or relationships are crumbling under the pressure. This book is for you, to support you and the difficult life-changing decisions you must make along the way. Please know you are not on your own.

I do not profess to be an expert, possess degrees, or have academic titles next to my name. My only accreditation is my degree in life. I will not mislead you by telling you I can make you rich or have all the answers. By sharing some of my experiences, I hope to help you understand your own abilities and develop new skills and opportunities.

To protect their privacy, I have changed the names of many of the people in my story. My old business colleagues will know who you are. You became my lifelong friends and the people I trusted to have my back. I thank you from the bottom of my heart for your support, sage advice, laughs, fun and tears we shared over the years. To the other fair-weather business associates who dropped in and out of my journey with their own agendas, this book is also for you. Hopefully, as a warning to others that there are many hidden agendas in business, and not all things are as they seem.

The creation of a business, finding markets, expanding a brand and using profits in responsible and ethical ways can sometimes turn into great adventures and, at other times, lead you into the pits of despair. I do not have all the answers. My story focuses on the essence of what it means to succeed in today's business world and the sacrifice it takes to make it or break it.

1. Four generations of Stacey's lived on Banaba early 1900s

CHAPTER 1

THE BANABAN CAUSE

Before my main business journey began, I had a Cause. It started back in 1990, with the discovery of a tin of old family photographs and documents dating back to the turn of the century. They were taken by my family, documenting their thirty years spent on Banaba, a remote tropical island in the central Pacific, called Ocean Island during colonial times.

This discovery led me on a quest to uncover the truth about this forgotten part of Pacific history. The island played a crucial role in Australia's development and wealth creation as a farming nation. Banaba, only six square kilometres in area, happened to consist of one of the richest deposits of phosphatic rock ever discovered.

I grew up with an eccentric great grandmother called "Little Granny" and my grandmother, "Big Granny". They enveloped me with their rantings while they reminisced about their lives on Ocean Island. My mother, who had been a child during the 1920s, only added to the chorus and kept telling me that I had to write their story.

I was not a writer! I had never been to Banaba Island. Yet, the three of them turned to me five generations later. Somehow the burden of responsibility ended up in my lap.

The photographs switched on something deep in my psyche, a realisation that all their stories were true. The images confirmed these people were real; they did exist, and somehow it was up to me to tell their story.

Over the years and research that followed, I wrote my first book about four generations of my family's lives on the Island and the impact of this significant discovery on the indigenous Banaban people. It was during this process that I fell totally in love with the Banabans. Their culture, their ancestral spiritual beliefs, their resilience and strength of spirit to endure all they had been through.

Finally, in 1992, I travelled with my mother and aunt to Rabi Island in Fiji to meet with the Banabans for the first time. The Banabans had been forcibly removed from their home by invading Japanese forces during World War II and relocated to Rabi in 1945, allowing the phosphate mining of their homeland to go unabated.

From the moment I first met the people, I knew I could not turn my back on them and just walk away. Every book about Banaban history had been written by ex-colonial government officials or businessmen who discovered the Island's great wealth in the rocks scattered across the ground.

It was through the elders' request that I worked with Banaban, Ken Raobeia Sigrah. We discovered we both shared the same passion for the Cause to seek justice and the belief that we wanted to right the wrongs of the past.

However, the elders had planned another mission for us – to find the ancestral skull of a Banaban warrior called Teimanaia, stolen from the Banaban homeland in 1933. Teimanaia's extraordinary feats are preserved in Banaban oral history. He is revered for his exceptional mythical powers and the protection of his people from various invasions and battles. More importantly, Teimanaia is believed to be the ancient godfather of the Banabans and represents the people's true origins and identity.

Generation after generation of Banaban descendants from the Te Aka clan had preserved Teimanaia's unusually large skull in a sacred *bangota* (shrine). Sadly, after discovering phosphate and subsequent invasion of thousands of foreign workers, the Island's company doctor would hear of the cultural and anatomical significance of Teimanaia's skull.

On 19 December 1933, the night before the doctor left the island for the last time, he tricked one of the Banabans into showing him the skull. After getting the young man drunk, the doctor took the skull and left the island, never to return.

From that moment in history, everything is said to have changed for the Banabans. In Banaban philosophy, only when Teimanaia's skull is returned to its rightful resting place back at Te Aka on the homeland will the prosperity return.

How could Ken and I ever refuse such a crucial mission? Over the years that followed, our quest to find Teimanaia would become an overriding commitment and pledge we both gave to Banaban elders in the 1990s.

Furthermore, Ken and I truly believed that our ancestors had somehow pre-planned our destinies. Now it was up to us, a century later, to do all we could to make a difference.

Our Banaban Cause was born.

2. In 1996 Stacey and Ken were asked by the Banaban Elders to work together to write their history.

CHAPTER 2

MY DRIVING FORCE

My Cause would bring about a turning point in my life and change my life forever. It would also create and become the driving force for my future actions in my personal and professional life.

The motivation of what drives us can come in many different forms. Even before I was lucky enough to find My Cause in life, I had an inbuilt drive to achieve or make things happen. It must have occurred at a really early age and, unknowingly, was part of my childhood. I soon discovered and identified what I was good at and the skills I did not have.

Two of my greatest assets were my creative brain and being gifted at birth with two amazing parents, who supported me and all my crazy ideas. But regardless of all their best intentions and support, they inadvertently influenced some typical childhood conditioning. There were only two children in the family. My brother, who was eleven months older than me, was clever with a very high IQ. I was the creative one in the family, not the "clever" one. I was the one with all the ideas; I took no pleasure at all from school or education, and much preferred being self-taught.

My father was a motor mechanic and a Staff Sergeant in the Australian Army; he spent his spare time on weekends rebuilding our small humble war service house into a beautiful family home. I was there by his side, helping hold the end of the timber he was cutting and watching him work his magic. My brother spent all his time with his head buried deep in books, becoming a human encyclopedia (we did not have computers in those days). My working-class father had committed a considerable amount of money to pay for a complete set of Encyclopedia Britannica, and my brother was totally absorbed in knowledge.

I was only interested in specific subjects at school. Otherwise, my mind shut off and I spent my school days daydreaming about things I could make or all the new ideas that came into my head. I was sent to an exclusive all-girls Catholic college run by nuns, where I was assessed as not being academically minded. Instead, I was put into the Commercial Class, which unfortunately had the letter "U" assigned to it. This step added to my conditioning, with the academic classes given the letter "A".

I found science interesting because it questioned my thinking, and history suited my inquiring mind. I hated English but loved writing essays as it let my creativity run wild. How could I ever have known then that my Commercial Class learning would provide me with lifelong skills that would hold me in good stead for my future business ventures? I left high school with high marks in science and home science, good touch-typing skills and basic bookkeeping.

At the age of fifteen, in the final year of high school, I set up my own business, crocheting shawls and tiny bikinis for boutiques, under the desk during Bible class. Demand grew for my items, and I worked late into my school nights to keep up with orders. My father was a well-disciplined professional soldier and a proud working man. He was concerned I would ruin my eyesight, and I would not keep up with the demand.

He made an interesting comment one night, that has stayed with me all my life. He said, 'You know to truly make good money, you cannot do it on your own, with your own hands. There are only so many hours in a day, and you can only really make money out of this business if you get other people to do the labour for you.' I was taken aback by his words, as he had no interest in business. At the time, he was a dedicated trade union man who was at total odds with the business world. Like many of us, we are used to putting in the hard work and what it takes, but sometimes that is not enough.

However, my parents were worried I was too trusting. I loved everyone. I did not like to speak ill or see bad in people. I must have lived in a bubble. Over the years, growing up, I was often told, 'You know you could make a fortune just out of your ideas.' I was always making money, usually using my creative skills and my own hands.

My mother, God bless her, became my agent, the marketing person selling my crafts amongst her friends. I was too busy working and creating goods to think about anything else, except for one new idea that came to the fore.

I wanted to buy a block of land. I turned my dream into reality when I found a newly developed housing estate on Brisbane's southern outskirts. I never realised how my previous negotiations with clothing boutiques for my goods would hold me in such good stead. I had confidence well beyond my years, and at fifteen years of age, I did look and act a lot older. The poor real estate agent I was negotiating with had no idea of my age until it came time to sign the contract. Legally I was underage, and my mother had to sign on my behalf. My dream had just become a reality and one of my first successful investments.

I assumed that running my own business and owning a suburban block of land was a normal part of growing up as a teenager.

I knew and understood I was creative. To everyone's surprise, my final school results divulged that there was a scientific brain hidden in there somewhere.

I gratefully left high school, ready to take on the world!

 LIFE LESSON: *Define what drives you and understand your childhood conditioning.*

I Wish I was Clever?

The word "clever" has so many meanings. I believe it can be confused and give mixed messages, some of which promote a more negative connotation such as "cunning" and "calculating". It can also embed our thinking with a label, that in my case was not easy to shake.

Was it my idea of not being the clever one in the family that provided the drive for me to work hard and achieve with my own hands? While, in contrast, I was not at all interested in my days spent at school.

"Clever" can also relate to more positive words such as "resourceful" and "imaginative", and people who are good at problem-solving.

Growing up, I had no understanding of what made me clever in my own right. Why am I putting such an emphasis on being or not being clever? I now find being told I am clever makes me feel good about myself. It makes me think that I can problem solve and create a business from just an idea. More importantly, it removes the negative label of "not being clever", which only limits my capabilities, ideas and decision-making. It is incredible to look back and realise that a simple word like "clever" can have such an impact on our thinking, our confidence and our self-belief.

Sometimes we can be our own worst enemy, shrouded in self-doubt with the labels we put on ourselves. Everyone is different and unique. None of us has been cut from the same cloth. Not all of us will become mathematicians, scientists or find the cure for the common cold. However, we may accomplish other equally important achievements in other areas.

In business, we often hear the phrase "we can achieve anything if we put our mind to it". While I agree with this statement, I also believe that we need to clear our minds first from the negativity and labels we carry. More importantly, we need to believe in ourselves and our own capabilities.

We need to acknowledge what we are good at and know what we are not good at. To build on our strengths and accept we are not perfect.

This valuable analysis will help us build inner strength and confidence. It will provide us with the essential armour we can carry in the business world and hold us in good stead in both the good and challenging times ahead.

By doing this self-analysis, we can find that the labels we inadvertently carry can become an asset, not a liability.

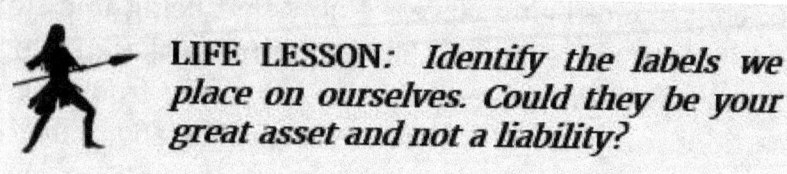

LIFE LESSON: *Identify the labels we place on ourselves. Could they be your great asset and not a liability?*

A "Light Bulb" Moment

When I was nineteen years old, and before I married, I moved to Sydney to be with my fiancé. It took me weeks of effort trying to find a job in such a large, bustling metropolis. I went for interviews every day, travelling miles across Sydney to some of the most industrialised areas I had ever seen. I was prepared to do whatever it took to get an office job. I soon found myself getting knockbacks every day. I had never experienced this before. What was I doing wrong?

I had never been so frustrated, then I saw this fantastic job in the newspaper. It sounded just like my dream job in one of Australia's leading advertising agencies. So, with nothing to lose, I applied. I could not believe it when I was contacted to attend an interview. The woman behind the advert was Catherine, an eccentric woman in her fifties, who looked like she had stepped out of a 1960s David Jones catalogue. Yet her modern office was at total odds to her old-world business glamour, hand gloves and all, and bright colours and other *objects d'art* adorning her desk and walls.

She also happened to be deaf while managing production on the creative floor of J. Walter Thompson, Australia's largest advertising agency. She advised me she had lost most of her hearing after contracting scarlet fever as a child; she relied on lip reading and written notes to communicate. We immediately bonded, and I could not believe it when she gave me the job as her assistant.

I had just landed my dream job. For the first time, I found myself surrounded by some of Australia's most wonderfully talented and eccentric creatives, and I had Catherine. She was so well-respected and loved in the industry, and she was my mentor. The whole creative team embraced being different, were totally unpretentious, and I absolutely loved my time working with Catherine and the rest of the team.

By 1981 I had left the wonderful career-filled life of Sydney behind. I was twenty-five years of age, married and living on our farm in the Gold Coast hinterland, surrounded by a myriad of animals. In the last week of January 1981, my first daughter, Riagan, was born.

Four weeks after her arrival, I took up a new challenge in life. Not only was I adjusting to being a mother, but I wanted to learn to defend myself and, at the same time, keep fit. I started karate classes. I was still breastfeeding, and my mother used to come along with me to my twice-weekly classes at the local Police Youth Club.

I didn't know what drove me to do all this, but I was hooked, and looked forward to the challenge. Maybe I had been away from my career and life in Sydney for too long? Over the next five years and now with my son Aidan, I spent my time raising two babies, looking after the farm, training and achieving my black belt in karate in the process.

I cannot tell you how hard it was to juggle it all, but the feeling of self-achievement was just amazing. Thank goodness for babysitters. It was up to me to learn and train to achieve my ultimate goal. No one could do that for me.

Growing up, I had always been self-conscious when people stared at me, or I was the focus of attention. I much preferred to stay in the background, working hard. I felt uncomfortable if I had to speak or appear on a stage. I was such a nervous wreck my knees would knock so badly I could hardly stand up. Karate changed all that for me. It provided me with excellent techniques – how to concentrate and stay focused. How could I ever have known then just how beneficial this would be in the years ahead?

When my son was two years of age, my isolated and busy life on the farm changed.

One of those "light bulb" moments was about to come into my life. This time it was Brian, an equally creative cousin who lived in Sydney.

He had studied stage and set design at the world-renowned Sadler's Wells Theatre in London. He returned to Australia to take up a role as a theatre set designer in Sydney and Brisbane. He went on to work in the film and television industry as a creative director with Australia's famous Kennedy Miller Productions. I loved his visits, and hearing about all the projects he was working on. It also allowed me more time to unleash all my ideas on him.

Brian was a kindred soul who seemed to understand me. But during one visit, I told him about another business idea – market the orchid flowers I was growing on the farm. He stopped me dead in my tracks. 'Stacey, whenever will you stop talking about it and just do it?'

His words shook me to the core; I questioned myself. 'Yes, Stacey, when will you go ahead and just do it?' So, I did. I immediately stopped talking and did it.

"Dial an Orchid" was born. It was a simple idea – marketing boxed orchid blooms I was growing on the farm. This idea led to the establishment of Anastasia's – the florist with a difference. I operated three shops in Orchid Avenue, Surfers Paradise, over the next seven years turning over $270,000 annually.

These seven years of running a rapidly growing retail business provided me with many experiences and life skills. I was unprepared for the speed and growth of the business, as everything I touched seemed to work and, as the old saying goes, "turned to gold".

I had never employed staff before or signed a lease, and knew nothing about company and business structures. I was good at ideas and building relationships with people and offering them personalised customer service. But the rest of the skills I needed to manage staff and overall finances were lacking. I had never experienced such high levels of stress nor the toll it would have on my partner at the time and our children.

When I eventually discovered that my flamboyant manager, Kelvin, was stealing from me, it was a devastating shock. An estimated $90,000 was unaccounted for.

In the 1980s, we didn't have EFTPOS machines and debit cards. It was a cash business that unfortunately provided a lot of temptation, especially when I didn't have the necessary checks and balances required for this type of business.

I was not only a nervous wreck but above all, I was hurt to the core when I realised I was being taken advantage of. I soon learned that when the wheels on the bus start to loosen up, the wheels will fall right off unless you act quickly.

Just as I discovered the depth of my loss, Kelvin had quickly exited the scene. He had a nice nest egg he helped himself to and all my customer records. He then added more hurt to my damaged soul and business by taking over the lease on the flower shop I was in negotiation about, at another location.

The whole episode was catastrophic and led me to levels of despair I never even knew existed. My trusting naïveté bubble had burst! There were days when I just could not drag myself out of bed to face another day. Luckily, my ex-husband, who was not involved in my business, encouraged me to stand up and fight and to take control of the situation.

I had to pull myself together quickly, and now it was time to put aside all my feelings, learn from my mistakes, dust off the hurt and lost money, and move forward. I never realised how the handling of these crucial events would become the catalyst to put me in good stead in later years. It would provide me with the essential skills to manage stress, learn the importance of business structure, and the importance of understanding my financial position daily. It also gave me invaluable experience in managing staff. And I realised that you cannot survive if you take everything to heart. Of course, this is a lot easier said than done.

This was a time in my life where I had just learned my first big lesson. Being in business was far more than just coming up with good ideas that people liked and wanted to buy. It was about learning to manage the monsters I was creating.

Another reality check came into my life right in the middle of this drama, that soon made me sort out my priorities. I discovered I was pregnant and, by January 1991, after working right up until her birth, Brynley was born.

Six months later, and with Brynley at work with me every day, I finally sold the business. I was worn out and ready to enjoy some time being a stay-at-home mum for a change. But again, things were about to change, this time, with my mother, Annie's urging.

My mother had worked with me for years, assisting me with the weddings side of my business. Over the later years of the business, we had a contract to supply flowers for Japanese weddings on the Gold Coast. The Japanese wedding business had grown rapidly, and we could have up to eight weddings a day in the peak season.

My mother insisted that I keep this side of the business when I sold out, and I reluctantly took her advice. At the same time, I looked forward to an extended family holiday touring the Australian outback.

3. Stacey with her father in their first shop in Lido Arcade, Orchid Ave, Surfers Paradise

One of the other key lessons I learned from this period after spending so much time and putting my heart and soul into my business was – time management. I had treasured my weekends away from the shop, where talk or reference to business and flowers were banned. It was the one thing in my business that I would not negotiate. It was my time to shut down, stop and spend time with my family and be mum. This simple time management principle would become my survival mechanism and one that I would continue in the busy and hectic years ahead.

Within the next six months, the Japanese wedding business was getting too much for Mum to handle, so I built a workshop at home and took over the business once again.

As the saying goes, "Mothers are never wrong"; this business was great and worked perfectly with my family's needs. I could source a lot of the material I needed from my gardens and our family's orchids we were growing. Brynley spent her early years as my little assistant helping me deliver my daily orders, and our Japanese colleagues loved her.

While I have not gone into all the details in this chapter, I hope I have provided a good understanding of what happens when you develop ideas, and they work. Before you know it, you can end up with a much larger business than you planned or imagined, especially when your dream was to work from home when your children are young.

For anyone thinking about entering the traditional retail industry, it requires long hours. Shops need to be staffed and opened seven days a week. Good management skills are imperative.

While my Japanese wedding flower business only provided an annual income of $35,000 a year, it was the perfect business to allow me to work from home. Depending on the bookings, I would do up the orders in the late afternoon when the children were home from school and deliver the orders by 8.30 the following morning. The rest of my days were free. It also allowed me to do large and better-paid private wedding flowers on the weekends.

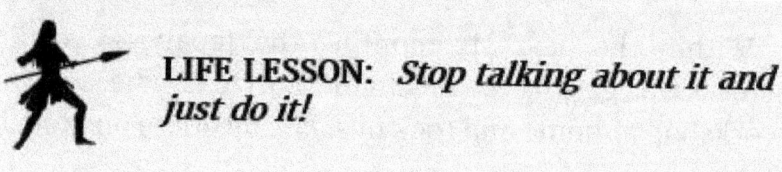

LIFE LESSON: *Stop talking about it and just do it!*

Reality Check – Poverty

I worked my Japanese wedding flower business from home for the next six years. It allowed me the spare time to establish and develop the Banaban Heritage Society, a not-for-profit organisation for the Banaban community living in exile on Rabi Island, Fiji.

During the wedding off-peak season, I spent time working and coordinating various television documentaries. Over the years, these included Sixty Minutes, Australia; NHK, Japan; ABC, Australia; and BBC, United Kingdom. This resulted in me spending time away from home, travelling extensively around the Pacific on these projects. By the end of 1997, life as I had known it up to then altered drastically.

To put it simply, my marriage broke up. One moment I had a home full of children, pets, and an angry partner; the next moment, I was out on the street with the money that was once jointly ours becoming solely his. The struggle over our children began. The life I once knew was over. I was permitted to take my clothes, computer, desk, and office chair. An old VW Beetle wagon with a board rack replaced my lovely Landcruiser. I never realised at the time just how handy that sturdy board rack would be.

I was unaware of the ramifications of allowing our family's accountant to put my Japanese wedding flower business under my husband's name. I was told at the time it was just for tax purposes to offset my husband's salary.

Before I knew it, all our joint accounts were closed, including access to my business account and the contract payments that arrived in my account each month. I was forty-two years of age, and I had just become penniless.

Divorce has a devastating impact on your life, your children, and your finances. Words cannot describe the emotional toll this takes other than to say that divorce, separation, and children affect your very soul. Sadly, there is no quick fix or magic solution. It is a situation you have to work through in your own way. However, as the adage goes, "time heals".

Of course, while all this is happening around you, it is hard to stay focused or worry about running your business. So, what did the experience of going through a divorce and suddenly becoming poor teach me?

First, divorce is an overwhelming issue when you work for yourself and do not have a full-time job to fall back on to pay the bills. Running your own business and having

4. We were so poor, and yet we were so happy! Stacey and Ken on one of their daily walks to Surfers Paradise 1997.

children means you have been out of the "normal" workforce for years.

Second, I had to make the heartbreaking decision to go on unemployment benefit for the first time in my life. This immediately put my confidence and self-worth at an all-time low.

Third, at the same time, I found that being in various businesses all my life was not an asset when it came to finding a job. I was over-skilled. I had done too many different things throughout my life, and my resumé obviously scared the hell out of prospective employers.

Again, my confidence hit zero. All those years, I had worked my butt off, strived to achieve, and yet no one wanted to employ me. I knew something had to give; I could not stay unemployed. Somehow, I found out about a government business training incentive, NEIS programme designed to provide you with the training to set up your own business. Ding! Ding! Did I hear the word "business"?

I came up with a new business idea, applied and got accepted. While I already had years of experience, the training course taught me how to write a business plan and prepare budgets to a level that could be pitched to a bank or investor.

I graduated with flying colours and started to receive an incentive payment, to run for the next twelve months. I set up my new business and left the long and winding road of the unemployed. The business idea I had started with was unviable, so I decided it was not worth wasting my time and money on the project. But how could I still qualify for my NEIS allowance?

Easy, I started to offer my new business and budget planning skills to others. Soon I had a consultancy business going and money coming in. I had just become a small business consultant and reaped the benefits of what I had learned during my NEIS training.

While this chapter sounds more doom and gloom, it also had a happy side. Ken arrived in Australia so that we could write our Banaban history book. Yes, they all assumed I was a writer. He came from his remote village in Fiji with just his small bag of a few well-worn clothes. His cousin had gifted him a brand-new pair of shoes, so he could board the plane and begin his new life in the hustle and bustle of the big city.

I picked him up from Brisbane International airport and squeezed into my tiny VW Beetle. From the moment we drove out of the airport, the car kept slipping out of gear. We made it to the Gold Coast before my little Beetle stopped completely, just short of a service station. Ken spent his first day in Australia pushing the Beetle down a busy highway into the service station, where he quickly looked at the engine and got the car running.

My hero, my knight in shining armour, minus the horse, had just come to my rescue. He was on a tourist visa and not allowed to do paid work. So now my $400 a fortnight NEIS allowance had to stretch to feed and support the two of us, pay the rent, and enough to pay for one tank of fuel for the VW. A double mattress for the floor, as I could not afford both a bed and food, food won out.

My first shopping trip to the supermarket was horrendous. By the time I hit the checkout with Ken in tow, the bill had reached $300. Ken's eyes bulged out of his head at the shock of what it cost to buy food in Australia, and from that moment he banned me from the weekly grocery shopping trip.

Ken was used to living on fish and rice, and he knew I was suffering. So, he saved the small packs of meat for me and went out fishing in the canals every night. He became well known by the children who liked to watch him and, in the end, taught a lot of them how to fish. This included my daughter Brynley. Meanwhile, I had learned a new skill – how to survive on just $400 a fortnight. We stayed in one room in a shared unit at Broadbeach and walked everywhere to save fuel.

He was missing his life back home, a life filled with his family, people, music, and laughter. I found all the free entertainment on the Gold Coast for the first time in my life and was amazed at what was on offer.

We walked to the Casino where they had great free entertainment, and during the night, we purchased one glass of cider that luckily came in a large glass. We shared the drink, sipping on it for as long as possible and enjoying the music and dancing.

Every morning we walked along the beach to Surfers Paradise to have our treat for the day: a one-dollar coffee we sometimes had to share, depending on the budget, and 20 cent ice cream. I had heard somewhere that it did not matter how broke you were; you had to be kind to yourself.

This became our daily treat; we sat on the busy street corner and watched the world go by. Ken vowed then, as we watched people all around us eating their food, that whatever happened in the future, we would return one day and be able to afford a meal.

Ken kept that promise to me. This episode made me appreciate the simple things in life, where possessions were more of a burden. The less I owned, the less I had to worry about, and the less I had to look after. We were so poor and yet so happy!

But how did I become a writer and acquire all the skills I needed? Of course, that's the easy part; I just had to learn them. Like most things in my life, I am self-taught; I rely on my stubborn determination and utilise my inquiring mind to learn and work out what I need to know to get the job done.

While I had done many business and other courses over the years, I had lacked interest in any type of school-based learning. I preferred to learn by burying my head in a product manual or online learning video, or step-by-step instructions with hands-on learning.

In the late 1980s my genius brother, Dan, had given me the old IBM XT computer he had built, which required my learning DOS coding. I worked hard to teach myself and drove him crazy with endless questions, until in the end, he refused to receive my phone calls.

He told me he could not cope with me being so dumb! In his eyes, I was definitely not bright. But he underestimated me – I was driven! Hurt by his words, and very driven by My Cause and my overwhelming need to use the darn thing, I plodded on.

Finally, I had built an extensive historical database of knowledge for the Banabans. I wrote my first book, relating to my family's thirty years spent living amongst the Banabans at the turn of the last century. And I built a functioning website all in my spare time.

By 1992, while the internet was still in its infancy and websites were just emerging onto the scene at a base rate cost of $10,000, I already had the Banaban website up and running. This quickly showed me the internet's reach globally and the excellent search engine capabilities. Our Banaban history and stories appeared on computer screens all over the world.

This effort, in turn, gave me a feeling of pride and personal achievement to spur me on. Just like the writing skills I'd had to learn, I had to get my thoughts on paper, or in my case the computer screen; speaking from my heart and learning the importance of communication. In turn, the Banaban Cause became a product that needed marketing. The Banabans needed their story told, and I soon found people around the world related to what I was saying and the words I was writing.

Through these developments, all driven by My Cause, the rest fell into place – the marketing, writing, communication and, above all, relating to people. All the skills that are essential for any business.

LIFE LESSON: *Remember when you hit rock bottom, there is only one way to go, and that is UP!*

5. Tribal Pacifica's success was going online and selling globally.

CHAPTER 3

GOD'S GIFT

By the end of the 1990s, I finally received a small property settlement which we used as a deposit for an apartment in a large complex with a single garage. By this stage, Ken and I both had full-time jobs, my youngest daughter, Brynley, still living at home, and now there was a mortgage to pay off. How could I ever develop a brand?

Our small garage became the start of our business empire. But how did it begin, and where did the original idea come from?

Life and destiny have a strange way of bringing people in and out of our lives when least expected, and events that change our lives forever.

One event became the trigger for what would become the new Coconut Revolution. While driving from Brisbane to the Gold Coast, what seems to have been a miracle saved my life.

After more than three years of doing various consultancy jobs in the natural health industry, I had a sideline business exporting Australian-made medicinal powders to an agent in South Korea.

At the same time, I worked a full-time day job for a large electrical firm where Ken had worked for some time. I was the only woman in a company of twenty-eight men. The business was flourishing, and I was managing the Company's office on my own.

Utilising my handy computer skills, I built and designed an automated database programme that helped me manage hundreds of different building sites at the touch of a button.

All those hours spent teaching myself on that old XT computer were paying off. I loved the challenge and the feeling of accomplishment, knowing my system worked well. It saved time and money, and I quickly had earned the respect of the men working there.

Because of my experience running my own businesses from a young age, I treated the job as I would my own business. I never took days off or had my usual lunch hours. But things were about to change.

Ken's adopted Fijian brother, Pat, had been visiting Australia and was flying out of Brisbane to return home. I had to give him an important parcel to take back with him, before he left.

I was already exhausted, as I used to work all hours of the night searching online for more export business opportunities and answering the mounting enquiries on my Banaban website.

I rang Rob, my boss at the electrical firm, and told him that I had to drop off something very urgent in Brisbane and would be back in the office by ten at the latest.

I could tell by the sound of Rob's voice he was not happy as his accountant was arriving that morning, of all days, and he needed me there. I drove to Brisbane through peak hour traffic on one of those hot summer mornings. The air conditioning in my car was not working, and it was a hell of a trip.

On arriving in Brisbane, I walked into a beautiful old Queenslander-style house where Pat was staying. The home's white walls were adorned with colourful Papua New Guinean paintings and large hand-carved tribal statues.

At that moment, I fell in love with the primitive and vivid art and everything that it represented. As I headed back to the Gold Coast, the images stayed in my mind, where I knew an annoyed Rob awaited my arrival.

My car's air conditioning was not working, and as the day's heat intensified, I had to leave the windows down. The hot air assaulted my face and eyes. I was travelling in the outside lane of the M1 with my cruise control set on 100 km an hour. Just as I neared the Mudgeeraba turnoff, I experienced a microsleep.

I was awakened by my car bumping over gravel on the side of the highway and realised it was heading towards the trees down the centre of the nature strip.

Quickly, I gripped the wheel and turned the car back onto the highway when it started to skid and spin out of control.

I do not know where the voice in my head came from, but I just held on tight and resisted every urge I had to try and right my car. I let the skid take control of my car and my life. My car shuddered, and I was sure it would flip over as it spun right around. I waited for the impact of the vehicles behind hitting me now that I was turned sideways across two lanes.

My life, as they say, flashed before me, and I felt a calmness come over me. I could not believe it when no one hit me, and I felt immediate relief that my car was still moving backwards at great speed. I was heading towards the embankment alongside the exit road. I noticed a small blue sedan and huge semi-trailer heading straight towards me.

Now I was going to be wiped out, and I had no control over my situation. Just as the small sedan was about to hit me, my car suddenly reared up over the embankment, and stopped instantly.

The small sedan hit the brakes and stopped a few feet from my boot, which was hanging out over the roadway. The concrete edge of the embankment had caught my car underneath on the fuel tank and lifted my back tyres just enough to leave them spinning in thin air.

As I sat there still gripping the wheel, a young man about nineteen years of age got out of the blue sedan and rushed to help me. All I could think was that he was the same age as my son, and I could have killed him.

It had indeed been a miracle. Except for the massive loss of tyre tread and a dent under my fuel tank, the car did not have a scratch on it. Other motorists rushed over to help me and marvelled at my driving skills, some commenting that they had seen the whites of my eyes and how miraculous it was – they were following me, saw what was unfolding and stayed back to avoid hitting me.

I had only put new tyres on the car two weeks before. They had hugged the road as the car teetered on the verge of flipping.

That feeling of losing control is something that stays with me. I give thanks every time I drive past that stretch of road, seeing crosses placed in memory of the people who never survived in similar circumstances to mine on that memorable day.

By the time I got to the office with the help of a lift from the tow truck driver, I was starting to go into shock.

The realisation hit me that day. I had to change my life, follow my passion and my dreams.

I knew I could not waste another minute. It did not matter how I would fund it or where the journey would take me. I had always felt blessed, but that day I truly understood what it felt like to be given the gift of life, and now it was up to me to make the most of it.

Within two months, Ken and I had both resigned from our full-time jobs. We re-mortgaged our home and headed off to the jungles of Papua New Guinea with $10,000 in our pockets, to buy a container load of beautiful native art and artefacts.

It was an unbelievable adventure from the razor-wired compounds in the dangerous capital of Port Moresby to the remote tribal villages throughout the northern province of Madang.

It was such an experience; spending time with the local villagers, learning about their unique culture and incredible artistic skills based on hundreds of years of tradition.

They possessed outstanding primitive skills using stone adzes, clay-based paints, and utilising the animals and plants from the jungle around them. They turned these into beautiful works of art, weaponry and essential household items right through to ceremonial clothing and objects. I learned the value of a dog's tooth necklace and the role of the old kina shell money as a 'bride price' that is still used in today's modern society.

My time spent in Papua New Guinea made me appreciate the beauty of the environment all around me. It gave me an appreciation of an ancient indigenous people who proudly upheld their traditions in an ever-changing world.

Another new business – Tribal Pacifica – had just begun.

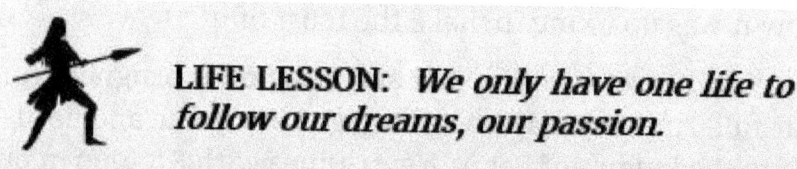

LIFE LESSON: *We only have one life to follow our dreams, our passion.*

Returning to a Harrowing Retail World

Ken and I returned to Australia with a container load of what I considered the most beautiful art and artefacts to sell. I went back to what I knew best, a retail shop.

Tribal Pacifica was established right on the beach in Surfers Paradise. We painted and decorated the shop to highlight our tribal products, and it was a store to be proud of. Tourists flocked to the shop, and locals dropped in to look and chat.

Our rent was $3,000 a month, but people were not buying. I soon learned that many Australians did not share my passion and had no real understanding or regard for genuine tribal artefacts. Overseas tourists seemed to appreciate it, but they were more concerned about being "overweight" on their return flights home.

I soon learned that posting the goods to my customers was their preference; this avoided customs and other issues when landing back in their countries.

I was busy online; searching for answers, trying to find markets where I could sell these beautiful items. We had a mortgage to pay, and both of us needed to make an income. I had to make my spur-of-the-moment investment decision work. Luckily, I had photographed every item we had purchased before we left Papua New Guinea.

Before the shipment cleared Australian customs, I had been busy using my handy database to catalogue our whole collection, and had built a Tribal Pacifica website. I boxed all the objects when they arrived and added a photographic label on each carton. I created small leaflets, each one stating that the item was a genuine, handmade, traditional product crafted from natural materials.

I soon discovered that eBay, a new form of online auction selling, had similar items on their overseas sites, mainly in the United States and Europe. They seemed to be selling quickly and bringing high prices, mainly in US dollars. In those early days of eBay, you could globally list your products in foreign currencies with just the click of a button.

Within days of listing the products, we were selling them all over the world. My cartons went from the far reaches of South America to Russia and beyond.

I was amazed at the value that collectors throughout the United States and Europe placed on my products, and yet here in Australia, they had proved a complete failure. Fortunately, I had only leased the shop on a month-by-month contract. We quickly closed our store, and a business friend rented us some storage space in his factory where we stored all our PNG stock.

Meanwhile, Ken received a phone call from his adopted brother, Pat, to ask him a favour. Pat had innocently led me onto this new business path. He ran various second-hand clothing businesses throughout Fiji, Papua New Guinea, and other Pacific Islands.

I heard laughter going on in the background, about a virgin and magic oil. Of course, the Pacific humour was at play, and after asking Ken what the call was about, I thought it wasn't important.

Pat was making some new type of virgin oil, and he wanted me to market it for him. But unbeknownst to me, Ken had arranged for Pat to phone me directly.

In Island custom, you cannot refuse a request from an elder, and Pat was Ken's elder. Ken could not say no, but being an in-law, I could. Of course, referring to me was a simple solution, and Ken would not lose face.

Pat took no time in phoning me. I tried to explain that I had no understanding of the product he was making and the oil's so-called magical qualities when he suddenly changed tack. He explained that he had set up this business just to assist the poor women in the village. To help them make some money to feed their families and assist with funding their children's schooling.

He knew he had me. He knew I could not say "no", as I worked on so many other Island aid projects over the years with the Banabans.

Another business had just fallen into my hands. One that I knew nothing about, and one I had no interest in. But if it helped the village women in some way, then my path was decided.

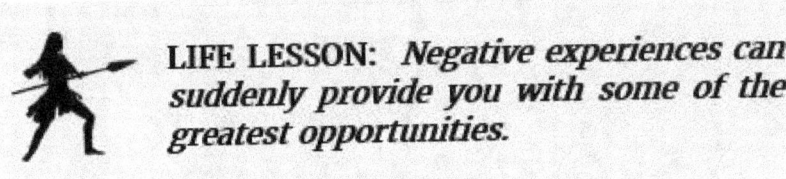

LIFE LESSON: *Negative experiences can suddenly provide you with some of the greatest opportunities.*

Turning a Cause into a Mission

We were flat out, shipping hundreds of boxed artefacts across the globe. The business had not only provided us with an amazing and sometimes scary adventure into far-flung villages throughout Papua New Guinea but also provided us with some hard-earned cash.

Things were too busy to think about Pat's Fijian magic oil project until the day that ten, 20-litre drums turned up on our doorstep. Ken immediately got excited, being reminded of his childhood where coconuts were part of his everyday life.

I was less enthused, being more absorbed with my ever-growing online Tribal Pacifica sales.

6. Where it all began. The Garage of Dreams

Now we had a total of 200 litres of virgin coconut oil sitting in our little Garage of Dreams. It took up so much room, and the car was sent to the driveway. I had the added pressure of quickly getting rid of the coconut oil and turn it into some money for the women back home in Fiji.

I had to call on all my creative juices and my overstretched imagination to develop a plan. The oil, I had to admit, smelled and tasted good. It reminded me of many of the trips I'd made to the Banaban island of Rabi in Fiji and how the women made the coconut oil and then dropped fresh flowers in the oil to provide different fragrances.

The Banabans covered themselves in this sweet-smelling oil, a substitute for deodorant, perfume, and hair treatments. I was always taken by how nice they smelled, and over the years I came home with various gifts of the oil.

I wanted to share that experience with people in Australia. A product that was natural and based on hundreds of years of tradition. But as it was, with fresh flowers dropped into coconut oil that had turned brown, it was not a viable option.

How could I commercialise this traditional product and get people to purchase it? At the same time, ensuring it was safe and not harmful to those with sensitive skin.

I researched the plants back on the Island and found commercial-grade fragrances based on the same plants.

We now had a way to reproduce our Island product to Australian standards, and the next step was choosing a name for our brand.

Of course, Ken came up with *Banaban* in honour of his people. At the same time, I suggested we should use this little bottle of traditional oil to help educate Australians about the plight of the Banabans.

Maybe it could serve a dual purpose? We could help the women back in the village and provide us with some much-needed funds to help fight Our Cause and take our fight for justice to a global audience.

I soon came up with a phrase for marketing the *Banabans*: "The Forgotten People of the Pacific". I designed brochures that have now been translated into more than ten different languages.

Over the next fourteen years of our coconut journey, every online order we shipped out would carry these brochures telling of the Banaban plight.

I had turned a product provided by Ken's relative, made by women in the local village and based on thousands of years of tradition, into a brand. How ironic, it was all based on the simple coconut, known as the "tree of life", that for centuries has provided the very essence of survival throughout the Pacific.

I was taken with the fact that a coconut could float across the ocean and land on foreign shores and then months later begin sprouting new growth to survive in a new land. I could not think of a more fitting and symbolic product to represent Our Cause.

I now became very interested in our new product, and my next consuming business mission had just begun. Next, I launched our small bottles of scented oil priced at only $4.50 a bottle.

There was no way we would make a lot of money at that price, but every label's message was far more important.

LIFE LESSON: *Whoever would have believed the simple coconut would become such a fitting symbol to represent our* Cause*!*

Garage of Dreams

Our Garage of Dreams had become our manufacturing plant. Ken quickly became the plant manager, and Brynley, our youngest daughter, his wayward assistant. She had just turned thirteen years of age, and no mother with a sane mind would want to launch a second new business and cope with a teenage daughter at the same time.

My happy naïve bubble was soon to burst; there was no turning back, and Ken's relative, Pat, was not about to let us revert to "island time". Before I knew it, another load of 200-litre drums had arrived, and they were stacked to the roof. Now I had to sell even more, and the pressure was on.

While we had been busy with the running of our retail store, I started to notice that the locals would come in to purchase my $4.50 bottles of scented oil. It was not enough to pay the rent and bills, but they were selling. At that price and with my new eBay online store being so active, I thought I would test the market with a few coconut oil listings.

Our tribal artefacts stock was going down fast, so I knew I had to start looking for more products to sell and keep that momentum going. Of course, I did not expect small bottles of coconut oil to sell, but they did.

I discovered that consumers in Australia, like me, had not heard of virgin coconut oil. People of the older generation remembered the old style of coconut oil as that greasy white stuff you spread all over yourself to get a good suntan. Obviously, the pretty flowers on the labels I designed and the pricing got the product started.

It was exciting that once people tried the product, they loved it and kept coming back for more. They were beginning to tell their friends, and our online sales increased. But the next step in our business growth was about to put a strain on our relationship. Pat had decided in all his wisdom that it was more economical to ship a pallet over to us with four 200-litre drums.

By the time he advised us it was ready and "on its way!" I was oblivious to what this would entail when it arrived.

This story may sound comical, but the enormity of this operation nearly shut down our small Garage of Dreams for good. I received a phone call from Pat's shipping agent, who wanted us to come and pick up our shipment that had landed in Brisbane.

Up until this stage, I was used to shipping items out, not bringing raw material in. I was now entering a whole new world. I look back and realise how much Pat had been spoiling us. He had been paying for and clearing our previous shipments through his regular shipping agents.

Once again, Pat had organised everything, but now we were told we had to pick up the shipment before it incurred storage fees.

With only our trusty VW beetle wagon, no idea of transport trucks, and four drums each weighing around

200 kg each, a plan was hatched with the help of my eldest daughter, Riagan and her mate, Greg, from down the road. He had a ute and was willing to offer Ken a hand. We thanked him profusely and took up the offer.

The Garage of Dreams was bulging with 20-litre drums and could not hold any more. My parents had a carport in the backyard for their boat, so we called on their help. Luckily for me, I could not go with the men to pick up the drums, but a few hours later, my parents were on the phone reporting on the drama unfolding at their home.

In theory, a ute, two strong men, and four drums sound like we had the situation under control. But no one thought of how the weight would affect the suspension of Greg's ute, driving down the M1 highway in peak hour traffic.

Somehow after a slow trip, they arrived at my parents' place only to face the next problem, how to get the drums off the ute. Ken, being a very industrious Islander, found some timber and boards to precariously roll the drums down out of the ute. Then he had to roll them through a garage and patio out the back to the boatshed.

The operation took them hours, and by the time Ken got home, he had lost it!

He gave me strict instructions to tell Pat that was it – this project was finished. Due to custom, he could not vent his anger at Pat. Still, I was given strict instructions that I had to tell him we didn't want any more oil, and he never wanted to see another 200-litre drum again.

Ken insisted he had no way to handle them, and now we had four drums stuck in my parents' backyard, miles away from where we lived.

While Ken was busy venting his concerns over the quantity and size of the problem, I phoned various business mates I had made over the years. One good-hearted soul, Ben, who was in the natural health industry, obviously felt sorry for me and agreed to purchase a 200-litre drum.

My excitement was at fever pitch, my first big sale.

Ken was more morose, as he had to get it out of the yard and onto a waiting truck. Meanwhile, I rang Pat in Fiji to share my excitement and made sure not to relay Ken's terse instructions.

After I finished gushing over the phone, Pat's deep voice on the other end replied, 'That's good, so how many drums can he take in a week? I have a 10,000-litre holding tank full of the stuff here on the farm.'

My excitement came crashing down. It had taken me six months to get this BIG sale, and I was deflated. That was a lot of small bottles I needed to sell.

Ironically, Ben continued to purchase just one 200-litre drum every six months over the next fourteen years.

His order never changed, and I never forgot the meaning of the first drum he bought from us and the journey that it led us on in the years ahead.

 **LIFE LESSON:** *The challenge of marketing a product that no one has ever heard of can become an amazing opportunity!*

Customers Where I Least Expected

The Garage of Dreams was now a hive of progress. Ken had two teenage assistants. One was his youngest daughter, Lusinta, who arrived from Fiji for a holiday and was soon roped in to lend a hand. They were now working all hours. Ken juggled his production with his part-time security job, mainly working late at night to help pay our mortgage and bills.

We had never realised that pure virgin coconut oil would start to solidify as soon as the temperature dropped below eighteen degrees. The oil had to be heated and melted before being poured into bottles.

Ken set up his small camping stove and a large stainless-steel pot as the key to his manufacturing equipment. It was another achievement on the road to mass production.

But the oil solidifying brought another problem with packaging, and how were you supposed to get the oil out while it was solid? The oil was so fine. Its density was less than water. When it melted, it leaked if the packaging was not totally airtight. So, a solution had to be found.

How do I market a product you cannot even get out of the bottle? How do I explain to customers that this is normal?

I remembered the old saying, "turn a negative into a positive". The long and frustrating process began by identifying this issue as a positive and proof of the oil's purity.

As the last of our tribal artefacts were listed for sale online, our sales of bottled body oils were doing their job and bringing in much-needed revenue. I realised I could not afford to lose the momentum I had already built online with my eBay store. I had to create more products to make our efforts viable.

A phone call from a young couple working in Darwin with Australian Indigenous communities would provide the solution. Before we knew it, they had placed orders for pallet loads of our scented oil for remote communities throughout the Northern Territory.

Now the Garage of Dreams production was running flat out. We found out that they only could place these large orders throughout the winter months. Summer in the north meant the wet season, and many of these northern Australian communities became isolated and unreachable.

Ken's camping stove and pot were no match for the thousands of bottles he had to fill. More vital equipment was needed. He already had multiple pots on the go, which put Ken and his wayward attendants under more pressure. I had to ditch the marketing and get on the production line.

But we did it!

The next problem: how do you get it to their Darwin warehouse? I became an expert on the phone, learning all I could about logistics. I found a trucking company that went to Darwin twice a week out of Brisbane.

Next, we had the semi-trailer with a tailgate lifter pulling into our apartment's narrow driveway blocking the entrance to our complex.

Sadly, the days of our Garage of Dreams were numbered.

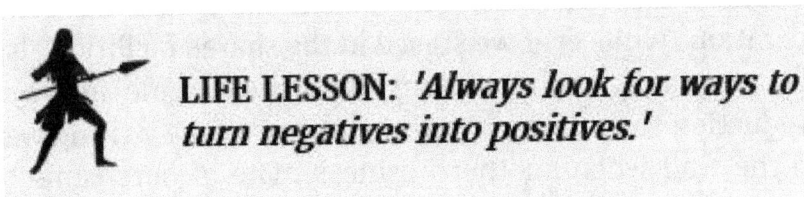

LIFE LESSON: *'Always look for ways to turn negatives into positives.'*

The Italian Connection and Swimming with Sharks

By 2007, we had moved out of the Garage of Dreams. Noel, a business colleague, had rented us warehouse space for our artefacts when our store closed, and he came up with a proposal.

He offered to set up a separate production room for us in his factory's food production area. This gave us a manufacturing room built to food standards and the extra storage we needed. It also provided us with the proper loading facilities for transport trucks and couriers. Everything went smoothly for the next eight months.

However, with the facility being shared, problems started to emerge. On a few occasions during unexpected visits to the factory, we found the factory's owner showing his prospective clients around our secured production area and discussing our business.

This began to ring my alarm bells. The factory owner Noel struggled with his own business and was really into manufacturing but had no idea how to sell or market anything. He started to copy some of the manufacturing processes of my other business colleagues.

There was no possibility of extending our business operations while ever we stayed in the shared facility. I also did not want people thinking they could come into our production room when we were not there. The writing was on the wall when another business mate of ours came to the rescue.

I had met him many years before while working as a consultant for another natural health company on the Gold Coast. Alberto was an Italian from Melbourne and a manufacturer who had been in the natural health industry for years. During our very first business meeting, we got talking. Before I knew it, I invited him and Nico, his Italian colleague, to our home for dinner.

Being Italian was what got my attention. My mother was crazy about cooking and entertaining people over dinner, and had become obsessed with everything Italian. She had even gone to the extent of taking Italian language classes in her seventies. She was so supportive of anything I did or asked. I roped her into producing a three-course Italian dinner with the promise it would be an excellent opportunity to try out her new language skills.

Dinner was a great success, and I realised my Italian friend had a wealth of experience in the import and export industry. He was old school, with a no-nonsense approach to business that I loved. He also amazed me with his skill of identifying business opportunities and developing products. His tales of turning food waste and by-products into viable natural products from fish powders, vegetable powders, and fish fertilisers enthralled me. I saw all the opportunities back in the Islands that were going to waste.

From that time on, he became a great mate. He loved my natural marketing skills, and together we formed a business collaboration. I began by finding my own clients in South Korea for his powders and developed regular export orders. He took me to trade shows in the United States to meet his clients and absorb the global trade opportunities.

Over the years of being in business, I found that being a woman put me at a distinct disadvantage in Australia. I came up with the ideas, and my male colleagues then claimed my ideas as their own and took all the credit.

The older Australian business generation was made up of men that I labelled "Neanderthal Aussie businessmen". It was like stepping back in time. They were in a time warp, and sadly many of the people I met or worked with had not one original idea in their heads. They used their wealth, power, and manipulation to steal other peoples' ideas, leaving many poor unsuspecting inventors or novices in their wake.

I identified the "Neanderthal" pattern early in my career. Still, I was shocked at how widespread it was and how it seemed to be the business norm. After all, as the saying goes, "it's not personal, it's only business!"

I have been at business dinners where ideas were raised over the meal, and by the following day, new companies were being registered to get the idea to market.

I soon learned the extent some of these opportunists would go to, and with my trusting nature, it felt as if I was swimming with sharks, and they were all circling.

Over the years that followed, our Italian colleague Alberto would often employ Ken. When he had large export orders, he flew Ken down to Melbourne to give him a hand with his production. We all became friends and enjoyed our time helping each other out. Money was not the driving force amongst us. It was the fun and adventure of it all.

When Alberto heard of our problems of sharing the factory, he was in the middle of buying the plant and equipment from a food-grade production set-up in Northern New South Wales.

He needed the machinery and thought we could use the wall panelling and some food processing equipment. Unfortunately, we needed a place to set it up in. He asked me to find an affordable factory, and then not only did he pay for it, but he also helped Ken set up the rooms to food standards.

Once up and running, he left us to take over from there. There were no loans, no commitment to paying him back or shares in our venture. We now had our first real Factory of Dreams, and a new stage of our journey was about to begin.

On a personal level, surrounded by an ocean of sharks, here I was teaming up with Alberto, an old-style Italian businessman from Melbourne. What could be more perilous?

In fact, it became the complete opposite. He talked to me like an equal, freely sharing his knowledge, and he became my mentor.

It was refreshing to go into meetings with experienced top industry American purchasing managers and to have the opportunity to learn from those experts. Being asked my opinion and what I thought was so different from what

I was used to in Australia. More remarkably, they listened to me and considered my ideas.

My South Korean agent treated me with the same respect. More importantly, he trusted me, and we developed an excellent working relationship over the years.

These opportunities provided me with the best lessons on my business journey. It taught me that if I did not want to turn into one of the sharks, business was far from being "not personal, it's only business".

If you wanted to be respected and build a solid foundation and network, it WAS personal and all about our relationships and the respect we shared.

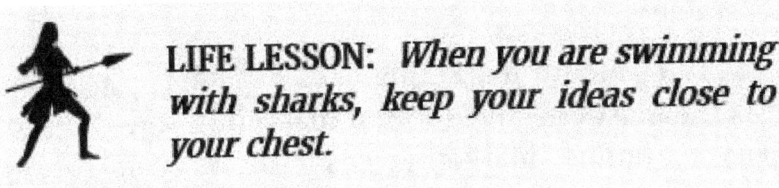

LIFE LESSON: *When you are swimming with sharks, keep your ideas close to your chest.*

A World at My Fingertips

As the business grew, so did the costs. The production crew's wages consisted of freeboard and lodgings. Ken, as production manager, was still juggling his security job.

At that time, the world of online selling, especially eBay and Alibaba, were still in their early days. Because of the international contacts I had already made implementing a Banaban web page back in 1993, I understood the opportunities.

I knew I had world access at the tip of my fingers. One of the best opportunities available was the search engine capabilities of these new emerging trading sites. Before I knew it, our products were appearing all over the internet.

As our products became more popular, we became recognised as one of eBay's "best sellers". People were contacting me to ask for my advice on how they could sell online.

In those days, most manufacturers relied on traditional sales channels: Manufacturing-Distribution-Wholesalers-Retail.

Online sales provided new opportunities for manufacturers to bypass all these channels and sell directly to customers.

Word of mouth marketing does not happen overnight but is the most effective form of marketing and at no cost. However, online marketing also allows you to offer discounts, bulk, and volume offerings with an excellent return on investment (ROI).

I had business colleagues in the natural health industry working at all different levels from product development, manufacturing, wholesaling, mail order and distribution. Their consensus was that once I sold a product online directly to consumers, I would not be able to sell to distributors or wholesalers.

This was becoming a concern as our small online business needed to generate $20,000 a month to break even and become viable. That was a lot of volume and online sales to turn over every month, especially if you had products that were retailing for just $4.50.

Feeling the pressure, I started to cry myself to sleep at night, knowing I was facing a near-impossible task.

But my gut instinct told me to hold my nerve. So, I made the difficult decision to stand my ground and not cave in to pressure and go down the perceived regular sales route. I remained fully committed to my dedicated online selling model. This was the new age of eCommerce, and I already saw the opportunities.

I could not believe it when other online traders complained about paying expensive listing fees and a percentage of their sales on these platforms. I replied, 'Where in the world do you get paid to advertise?' They could not see the bigger picture of what they had available to them at the tip of their fingers!

The new online auction sites allowed us to make money and provided marketing and advertising capabilities that the best advertising agencies only dreamed about.

Our products were now popping up on computer screens all over the world. At the same time, I was using our listings to educate the public on the benefits of coconut oil and the plight of the Banaban people. Online sales not only gave us better margins but, more importantly, direct contact with our customers. Their feedback was invaluable, and so was their support.

I soon realised we were building an army of coconut followers who loved our products and told their families and friends about them. They believed in Our Cause and what we were doing to try and make a difference.

Our customers embraced the Banaban traditional way of life that relied on the coconut as their "tree of life".

7. A busines started on $4.50 product and based on thousands of years of tradition.

They began to appreciate Pacific culture, and like all things "Pacific", they became part of our extended family and very much a part of our journey.

I kept telling myself that once we lost that personal connection to our customers, we would be just like every other company. I wanted our business to be different. I did not want to follow the usual route, even if, behind the scenes, I could not sleep, stressed to the max about how I could fund it and how I would pay the bills.

I held my ground with a little help and support from some great business colleagues, but more on that later. Things were about to change with our product development. Our new Indigenous Australian consumers had taken a real liking to our body oils throughout Australia's remote northern regions. Now they were asking us to manufacture other body products for their communities, such as body butter and coconut soaps.

Our coconut oil was so pure, with just minimal processing. In Fiji, the coconut farm used gravity to filter out the heavier coconut particles while the oil was in the settling tanks, resulting in a fine layer of sediment left behind. Not wanting to waste this part of our oil, I had already developed new markets for this sediment.

Coconut soap was our first, but soon we had the horse and stud cattle breeders contacting us. Next, the raw food enthusiasts heard about us and wanted to buy these coconut-rich dregs.

Initially, I developed a whole range of fruit-flavoured body butters for our Indigenous Australian consumers. These included strawberry, pineapple, lime, coconut, banana and two others – Australian lemon myrtle based on traditional medicine, and the last, "fragrance and colour free". This body butter was suited for people with sensitive skin and other skin conditions.

I kept the range as chemical-free as possible and used natural vegetable food dyes to produce lovely looking and smelling body butters. Unfortunately, the formula had to be adapted to withstand the high temperatures throughout the region.

The first casualty was the natural food colouring which had to be removed. The colourings reacted with the virgin coconut oil and, combined with the heat, were causing the coconut butter formula to separate.

We soon learned that when working with such fine pure oil, there was no guarantee that it would work like standard coconut oil in formulations. We were forging new ground in our product development, and it was all a bit of a trial and error to get it right in those early days.

Many of our mainstream customers started to request more food-grade virgin coconut oil as a healthy oil alternative. I realised I had to take advantage of the opportunity and develop more size and packaging options to expand our food range.

Our online marketing, which was virtually free at the time, was starting to build momentum. The next major step was developing our one-litre jar product. It took me months of searching Australian packaging manufacturers before I found a suitable container.

Glass jars were commonly used as packaging in the food industry. Still, it was not a good option for online sales due to the difficulties of weight and breakages when shipping glass.

There was another major consideration: pricing. I kept hearing the words of one of my consumers telling me how much she loved virgin coconut oil. Yet, her husband said it was too expensive for daily use, and he wanted her to keep it for special occasions.

This was the exact opposite of what we needed. We needed volume turnover, and I needed to make our oil affordable. Until that stage, the only coconut oil on the market was priced over $30 for a small jar. I came up with a $19.50 price point for our new one-litre plastic jar and launched it on the market.

With the introduction of this new product, sales took off at lightning speed. To optimise these online sales and accommodate Pat's request to turn over more volume, I introduced multi-buy bundles: two, three, five, one-litre jars. Again, I discounted the pricing based on the more you bought, the better the price. I also made the bundle packs to suit the best shipping price options on offer.

Next, I introduced large wholesale cartons offering 24 jars weighing just under the 25 kg limit for couriers. Before I knew it, our regular customers were buying bulk cartons, and coconut oil flew out the door.

 **LIFE LESSON:** *It takes courage to hold your ground and go against the norm to develop new ways of doing things.*

8. The development of the first one-litre jar and combining Banaban tradition with the products was crucial Ken's niece Geness Mau became the face of our brand.

CHAPTER 4

SLEEPLESS NIGHTS

By 2008, the new Factory of Dreams was an exciting development. Ken's two wayward assistants, Lusinta, who had arrived from Fiji again to help us, and Brynley were flat out.

At the same time, Ken was juggling increasing orders, production and raising our two teenage daughters. By this time, Brynley had her first boyfriend (who shall remain nameless), and he became an added factor and distraction in the whole equation.

Ken had acquired a great new holding vat capable of holding 200-litres of oil, to assist in speeding up his bottling process; his first real step towards a proper commercial operation. It was what they called a double-jacketed stainless steel vessel. You filled water into the outer tank and then heated it. It melted the oil perfectly and allowed it to flow without burning or overheating.

Brynley's boyfriend was keen to help, and with his background in food handling, we accepted his offer. Only a few months after Ken's "pride and joy" had been running flat out, he asked the boyfriend to fill up the tank one morning with oil and water so he could get production running for the day. Ken had to run off to do an errand, and I was upstairs clicking away online.

I had no clue what was going on downstairs when I heard an explosion. Brynley and her boyfriend were running into the production room. Obviously, they had taken a break outside.

There in all its glory was the mangled wreck of Ken's "pride and joy"! I began sliding across the floor, awash with 200-litres of sweet-smelling coconut oil. Apparently, Brynley and her boyfriend had a bit of a tiff. He had followed Brynley outside to try and make amends. Meanwhile, the water had been left turned on. With pressure building and nowhere to escape, the vat exploded.

Ken returned to find the disaster, a very worried and apologising boyfriend, Brynley ducking for cover and me near tears. All I could see was the loss of a machine we had spent thousands of dollars on, and we had potentially $4,000 worth of lost orders.

In his "Island way", Ken was much more forgiving than me, and after a day of cleaning up the mess, he announced that his "pride and joy" was beyond repair. It was back to square one. We survived the setback, and with the boyfriend's days being numbered, he finally disappeared.

Meanwhile, I was facing mounting bills, and irregular and erratic sales that can only be described as nerve-wracking. Whenever I started to feel we were wasting our time, and it was time for us to look for real jobs, sales came flowing in. Ken had a strong spiritual belief in talking to his ancestors.

Since his arrival on the Gold Coast, this meant visiting the Burleigh Heads headland to connect with his ancestors as the sun rose over the vast expanse of the Pacific Ocean. It was his special time and one that gave him the strength to continue the path we were on.

He knew I was crying myself to sleep, tossing and turning all night worrying about how I would pay our bills. He assured me money was coming, and to my amazement, money or sales turned up when we most needed them.

After a challenging first twelve months in the new Factory of Dreams, I was at the end of my tether. All the hours of hard work, and we could not crack the $20,000 monthly turnover figure that my wonderful Greek accountant, Con, told me would turn things around. One day in my office, I poured my heart out to him, telling him I was thinking of selling the business.

I had given it everything I had, but I had to be practical. Was I just wasting our time and efforts? I had to make a decent income that would pay our mortgage and help feed us. I was not greedy, but a roof over our heads and food to survive was becoming an absolute priority.

Con had been with us from the beginning and knew exactly where I was coming from. He turned to me and calmly said, 'Stacey, if you give up now and sell your business, someone is going to walk in here and reap the benefits of all your hard work.' He added, 'You are getting close to your break-even, and once you hit that, everything will be different. Just try and hold on a little longer.'

The most important thing he told me that day was that he believed in what we were doing, and we could do it!

His reassuring words of advice and support hit me like a brick and stayed with me, giving me the strength and a glimmer of hope as we hovered close to breaking even.

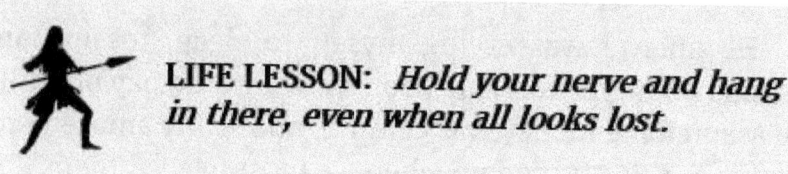

LIFE LESSON: *Hold your nerve and hang in there, even when all looks lost.*

Being in Demand

Sometimes you hear people talk about timing and stars all aligning, or in our case, a Cause that kept us focused on the bigger picture. After being in the new Factory of Dreams for a year, we realised that we had to build a second floor to expand our storage area. With the Easter break and a helping hand from Ken's daughter's boyfriend, Peter, the two of them got the major refit underway.

Our factory's entire contents, including all the timber and materials needed for the refit, were moved out into the car park. There was nowhere to secure it at night, so it all had to be gathered up and stored back in the factory at night. They had thrown stuff everywhere, including the processing room floor, and my organised mind went into meltdown.

I was there to give them an unwelcomed hand and keep my online sales going over the Easter break. I had found out that during holiday periods, people liked to go online and purchase.

While the whole factory was in chaos, I received a phone call to ask if I had seen a story about coconut oil that appeared on Channel Nine? With everything going on at the factory, I had missed it but had noticed the sound of my eBay online cash register going off.

I heard the sound continuing through the construction noise and thought I had better check what was happening. I found about fifty sales sitting in front of me, with more coming as I browsed through them.

I then went online to view the Channel Nine television story my friend mentioned. It was a whole segment on the "new age" health benefits of virgin coconut oil.

A naturopath featured in the programme just happened to be holding a jar of our oil. The strong blue island label I had designed was doing the job. It caught your eye and made our brand pop out on the screen. We had just received about $30,000 worth of free advertising.

As I tried to explain this to Ken, he dismissed it, too busy and focused on the construction.

I had heard nightmare stories where companies had a story appear on television about their products only to find themselves completely overwhelmed and swamped with orders. They instantly became victims of their own success, as people complained they had taken their money and orders and never received the goods.

These thoughts kept running through my head, so I decided to hatch a plan. I had to take full advantage of this fantastic opportunity and not let it turn into an utter fiasco that could destroy us completely.

Luckily, Ken had built up some stock the week before, and I had purchased a reasonable stack of courier and express post packs.

While the express packs were far more expensive than the couriers, I knew I had to use this option. They were the best option for long-distance deliveries, and I could not worry about the profit margins.

From what I was finding, this story had gone Australia-wide. So were the orders coming in. With the Easter break, there was a four-day delay to dispatch orders.

If I left everything until the factory was back up and running, there could be another week of delays.

First, I cleared enough space among the chaos downstairs. I grabbed the large one-metre empty cartons that our one-litre jars came in from the manufacturers. Four of these cartons fit perfectly on a pallet.

Next, I started to compile the orders and designated each carton to a courier, express post and even long-distance states such as Western Australia, Northern Territory and Tasmania.

For two days, I filled orders but started to run out of stock. I tried to pull Ken away from his renovations, but he told me the orders had to wait. I knew he was on a mission to get the factory back up and running by the end of the Easter break, but all I could see were more orders piling up.

Pallets filled with packed orders were now taking up more room on the limited cleared space I had on the floor. I told Ken if he could not fill more bottles of oil, I would have to do it. He again ignored my pleas, so I began clearing space around our filling and labelling machines.

I had never worked on these machines before but thought it could not be too difficult. After setting everything up and moving large 1,000-litre totes into the production area, my new oil bottling and production skills began.

Every time I asked Ken for advice or assistance, taking him away from the building, he became increasingly annoyed.

Surrounded, with chaos all around me, I spent all day filling, sealing and then labelling bottles before jumping back into packing orders.

By the time Easter was over, I had hundreds of orders ready to ship out, and Ken's new renovations were complete.

It was time to look for a staff member (outside the family) to work full time on dispatching orders. Our sales for the first time went well over our break-even figure.

I rang Con, to tell him the exciting news. I yelled, 'We did it!' I had to share my excitement with him. Without his words of encouragement, we never would have gotten there. I patiently waited to see if this would be a one-off event.

LIFE LESSON: *Don't let an opportunity make you become a victim of your own success. You need to do whatever it takes to make the opportunity work to your benefit.*

The Curse of Cyclones

Our sales began to skyrocket as word-of-mouth referrals led to more new customers. I was excited to see the number of repeat customers who kept coming back for more. It was only then that I realised we were on to a winner and people loved our products.

We not only hit our break-even point, but sales kept growing rapidly. While all this was happening, another major problem threatened to derail everything.

Tropical Cyclone Tomas had wreaked havoc throughout Fiji's northern region, and our coconut farm was impacted. Usually, the farm produced between 16,000 and 20,000 litres of oil every two months, enough to fill a 20-foot container. In the export industry, the imperial unit of measure is quoted when referring to the size of export containers.

We had never needed to buy that much, but with sales growing, we needed to increase our stock levels. I had Jone from the farm on the phone. He predicted his production would drop back to about 4-5,000 litres a month until the coconut palms fully recovered.

Just before TC Tomas had hit Fiji, the other major coconut oil-producing country, the Philippines, was devastated by a typhoon. About one-third of their coconut farms and production had been wiped out.

After working so hard to build the demand for our oil in Australia, I could not believe that our supplies had been reduced so substantially.

I now faced another stressful situation that challenged me like no other.

LIFE LESSON: *In business, there is always something that will challenge you, and learning how to manage stress is essential.*

Turning a Negative into a Positive

After years in business, and having to learn to manage stressful situations from an early age, I had not realised I had become an expert juggler with money, cash flow, customers and suppliers. This stood me in great stead for never missing an opportunity.

Even with the bad experiences with staff in my flower business, I now had a different attitude towards managing stress. Yes, during the early days of our coconut business, I still went to bed at night and cried my eyes out, but that was the only time I allowed my fears to stand in the way.

I also had Ken behind me talking to his ancestor in the early hours of the morning. At the same time, Con hovered in the background, keeping me calm with his encouragement.

Con's projections proved correct. But now, I had a major supply problem to deal with and ensure it did not sink our business overnight.

My brain went into overdrive, thinking about how I could manage it. The farm could produce four 1,000-litre totes (bladders inside cardboard outers), also referred to in the industry as flexitanks, per month from their limited coconut supply.

I just had to get us through this drama from the cyclone damage until the next growing season.

Jone, the farm manager, had already advised me that the new undamaged coconuts were already on the trees. But we just had to wait for the fruit to grow to maturity and drop on the ground again for full production to be back on.

Every time I was on the phone with Jone and heard his words, 'six to twelve months', my heart sank. I couldn't help fixating on the negatives and all the reasons why we could not survive this.

I have another close business colleague who has always told me, 'Out of every negative, there are positives.' Okay, it is not always easy to find the positives, but they are there somewhere amongst the problems you have no control over.

I had to put aside my negative thoughts and not waste time or energy worrying about what could **not** be done. I had to focus on what **could** be done. What could I do to make us survive the next few months until Mother Nature stepped in to rectify the damage?

I decided that I had to get the first 4,000 litres of coconut oil over as soon as possible. I couldn't wait four to six weeks for the next ship to leave Fiji. I got on the phone to my shipping agents in Australia and Fiji and asked for quotes to ship the four totes of oil via air freight.

It sounded like a simple request, but with the total shipment weighing 4 tonnes, I soon found out that only the bigger airlines had the capacity to carry this type of freight. Qantas was my first port of call, but their quote was expensive.

Luckily, Air New Zealand came to the rescue and was happy to add our shipments to their backload coming via Sydney. We had just saved ourselves $3,000 on the Qantas quote.

With the virgin coconut oil industry still in its infancy in Australia, these types of oil shipments had never been done before. A shipment of 4 tonnes on airfreight is not cheap. In fact, instead of costing just $1,000 for a full container on regular sea freight, I was looking at about $8,000 on airfreight. This equated to at least $2 extra per litre on freight alone.

While this was going to impact our profit margins, there was still a small profit nonetheless and a happy, ever-growing customer base.

So, the first of our many air shipments began. But of course, nothing is that simple, and some other negatives and setbacks reared their ugly heads. The first one was that I had to prove to the airlines that the oil shipment was not dangerous goods, and not highly flammable. That is not easy to prove when it is oil, but my Safety Data Sheets worked; another skill I had learned from my import-exporting experience with Alberto.

The next challenge was having to truck our four pallets across from Suva to Nadi airport on the other side of the island. Our shipments usually connected with inter-island shipping in Suva, and we exported directly from there. But airfreight had to leave from Nadi, on the opposite side of the island.

Anyone who has been to Fiji will know that road travel across the island is not always an easy task at the best of times. Just finding a truck capable of holding 4 tonnes at a time was not possible. We had to rely on breaking up our shipments just to get them onto local trucks. It also was proving another added expense.

On the third shipment, we struck new problems. This time it was the airlines. Luckily for us, Air New Zealand had been very supportive until two of our 1,000-litre totes had started to leak.

We were unsure if this was caused by the overland trucking, careless forklift drivers or something else. It was only through the grace of God that the leaks were not noticed until they arrived. The totes had to be wrapped up in plastic to prevent more oil from escaping.

Coconut oil melts into a very fine liquid once the temperature rises over 18 °C, but while in the air, the temperature drops to 7 °C and below, so our large oil totes would set solid.

I believe this was the one saving grace with our leaking shipment. Our shipping agents kindly warned us that the airlines were threatening to ban our future shipments unless these problems were resolved. It could end up being the final nail in the coffin.

The leaking shipment finally arrived at our facility in a real mess, but thankfully, we could salvage enough oil to continue and make up our orders.

We discovered that the timber pallets had nails popping up, piercing the bottom of the totes—the continued battering of bumpy Fijian roads and rough handling by forklift drivers did not help.

To overcome the problem, the farm was able to reinforce the bottom of the totes with more packaging and add additional nails to the pallets. We also had the farm place each of our totes in a large heavy-duty plastic outer bag to prevent oil from escaping.

This was finally the last of the problems we had overcome, and our customers never realised the pressure we were under behind the scenes.

We created and built our business on the back of a devastating natural disaster.

The day I received a phone call from Jone on the Fijian farm to say that the trees were heavily laden, it was music to my ears. The coconuts were starting to drop everywhere, and the processing plant was running twenty-four seven.

LIFE LESSON: *Your customers never need to know of all the drama and problems going on behind the scenes. Just keep a smile on your face and the products on the shelves.*

9. Creating a strong brand image that makes yourproducts stand out from the rest.

CHAPTER 5

DON'T MISS THE OPPORTUNITIES

One of the most important aspects of entering the business world is being able to identify opportunities. They can come in many different forms. For me, I believe I saw the world differently.

Years ago, while purchasing tribal artefacts to bring back to Australia from Papua New Guinea, we had stayed with one of our Island relatives. She was a lecturer residing at one of the universities in Port Moresby.

She asked me to give a talk about my experience, for students studying for a business degree. I had no time to prepare a proper lecture or training notes, so I kept my presentation general.

What had impacted me during my stay at the university compound was the beautiful gardens and trees. They opened the gates every Sunday to the public for a Farmers Market, and it was popular and successful.

My audience were all young PNG locals keen to enter the business world, so I focused my talk on identifying opportunities. During my time spent working and visiting local communities around the Pacific, I was always taken by the abundance of natural resources and the beautiful products made within these communities.

I gave my observations and told them that, as I walked around the university's grounds, I noticed the trees were heavily laden with mangoes.

That made me immediately wonder what was happening to all the mangoes. Were they given away to the local communities, were they just being left to rot on the ground or were they used to produce a product for a business venture?

So much abundance, so much going to waste, and so much lost opportunity.

As I voiced my ideas and thoughts and discussed the unique crafts and products produced at village level, I saw the students' "light bulb" moment.

Here they were, living amongst so many natural resources they took for granted that could be developed for western markets. Australian consumers craved healthy natural products and a connection to genuine handmade products.

The real challenge was to identify the products and then to see if they could be commercialised.

If they could, the next step was to see what processes were required to bring the product successfully to market.

I would like to share an excellent example of this from Alberto. He is an expert in this regard. He told me a story years ago regarding the disposal of waste from one of Australia's largest fish markets. It was a big issue for the fish market management and the local municipal council to dispose of the fish waste.

Alberto's fellow Italian business associate became aware of the problem and saw it as a good opportunity.

He approached the local council and offered his services to remove the waste and suggested that the local council charge each trader a waste disposal levy.

The council soon worked out his offer was far better than their existing costs and signed a contract. The council then introduced the levy for the traders, and Alberto's business associate started to pick up the waste.

Alberto's friend had just set up a new supply source for his liquid fish fertiliser business, with the bonus of being paid to pick it up. I thought how clever he was to see that opportunity, and as they say in business, the rest is history.

While most people would have overlooked fish waste and concentrated on the cost of disposal in land waste, he saw it as a business opportunity.

Like many migrants to Australia over the years, they identified the opportunities and created new industries and markets, taking full advantage of what Australia had to offer.

Another interesting example of turning a production problem into an opportunity is the development of the Banaban community virgin coconut oil project back on Ken's Island in Fiji. I used to take our small bottles of scented oils back as gifts for all the family and found they were very popular.

Over the years that followed and the hard work and dedication of key women in the community, a local coconut oil factory was established.

The Fijian government was very supportive of the project, especially when they saw the export trade figures on the amount of coconut oil our company imported to Australia.

Initially, when the project was set up, we assisted with some equipment and training, and similar to our Australian operations, the women began by producing scented oils.

We had thousands of old labels that had old addresses on them. With a simple over label hand-applied on the Island, we donated thousands of dollars of labelling to the project and the same plastic bottles we were using in Australia.

The Island community loved the commercial fragrances we were using, which I had based on the flowers they used traditionally. We donated fragrance for the first two years of the project, costing over $100 per litre. This allowed the project to begin with a solid foundation, based on popular products now being handmade by Banaban women living on the Island.

Most aid-based projects collapse after a few years when the funding dries up and support is withdrawn. So, it was essential for the project to survive; it had to be sustainable and well managed.

It is not easy to say "no", but I knew if the project was to survive, I had to withdraw support so eventually, they could stand on their own feet. I did this slowly as I knew each step was not easy for them.

First, I told Terikano, the project's manager, that purchasing the plastic bottles made in Australia wasn't viable. She was keen to keep up with the same supply.

After paying for a few shipments, Terikano realised the cost of the bottles in Australian dollars, the export shipping, plus Fijian import duty was just not viable.

This convinced her that they had to find a bottle supplier locally in Fiji. After stressful days of searching down on the main island of Viti Levu, Terikano was able to source local bottles, and the problem was overcome.

In some cases, the labels I had supplied them had to be cut down, but they made it work. Over time with the different sized bottling they had to purchase, they had to design and make their own labels.

This gave Terikano another new challenge that she overcame; this assisted her and her team in developing new skills.

The issue of the expensive fragrance was the next challenge. It ended up being one of the project's best opportunities. On one of my visits to the Island's facility, I encouraged them to identify local plants on the island, especially those used traditionally over the generations.

I discussed with Terikano and her team the idea of making their own flower and plant infusions and extracts. They became very excited, and before I left the island, some of the staff had already identified fragrant plants and started work on this new idea.

Their efforts have proved very successful. More importantly, they have developed products based on their traditions that are genuinely unique to their Island.

The project is moving forward with assistance via the Fijian government and other Pacific trade organisations, assisting the entire Island community in achieving certified organic status.

This process will provide even more opportunities when all their products become certified as organic.

From all the problems this project initially faced, through the sheer determination and management of Terikano and her enthusiastic team, solutions were found. The project has not only proven sustainable but has become the model for other Pacific communities.

It shows what can be achieved, and can genuinely make a difference to enrich so many lives.

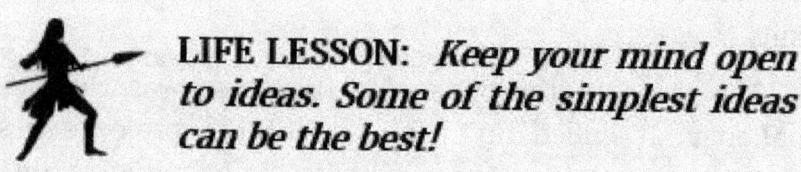

LIFE LESSON: *Keep your mind open to ideas. Some of the simplest ideas can be the best!*

Creating a Brand

I never realised I was good at creating brands or overall product concepts until I had people commenting on our *Banaban* coconut oil branding. I even found out that they were using our brand and business model as a case study for a university course on marketing. I was taken aback but smiled on hearing this.

Luckily for me, branding concepts were something that came naturally. Maybe working in Australia's leading advertising agency at the young age of nineteen influenced my thinking without me even realising it at the time.

However, coming up with business names and ideas had been part of my creative thinking since my first business in my school days.

I had found my brand concept for my flowers shops was different from what was around the Gold Coast in the 1980s. I had always used tagline slogans, and for the flower business, "Florist with a difference ..." summed up precisely what the business was about.

I had carried the concept through in every flower design, staging, shop design, even through to our staff uniforms.

When I purchased my new shop, it was set up like a typical old-fashioned traditional flower shop. I was lucky enough to meet with a leading interior designer from Sydney and asked for his advice. He suggested painting all my shops black. He even wanted me to blacken the ceilings, let my flowers stand out, and create drama in my shops. It was a bold suggestion in the eighties, but I thought what he said made sense.

The black theme worked perfectly with my black business cards along with specialising in such bold and vibrant tropical flowers; it only added to the drama of my tagline. So, the theming, grouping, and consistent branding became a key focus from that point on in my business career.

Whenever I came up with a business idea, I found coming up with a business name was the next important step. I didn't realise the importance of a brand name compared to a company name in the early days. Usually, I registered a simple business name, but it was a different story once I began to register companies.

A company is a legal entity that usually owns the brand name and can have different owners and shareholders over the years. The company can also own multiple brands. Likewise, a brand can be sold multiple times but still retain its reputation and standing within the marketplace.

The brand name can become a valuable asset that can be traded over the years.

Here are some tips that I hope will help you with your brand development:

Overall Concept

This is the most important aspect I consider first. What is your business about? What products or services have you developed? What is the projected customer base you are targeting?

Brand Name

Does your brand name reflect what your products are about or the services you do? Does your brand name appeal to your customer demographic? For example, our brand name represented our important Cause and, therefore, the key message we wanted to publicise.

I suggest you keep the name simple. Write your brand name suggestions down on paper and see how they look in print. Will the name look good on your labels, on your website, etc.? If you are also targeting overseas marks, how will the name translate into other languages?

Brand Slogan/Tagline

It is an advertising phrase used to express the importance and core idea of your product or service. Keep your slogan short and simple, no more than seven or eight words at the most. It should tell your story and, at the same time, be catchy. Include your tagline in all your marketing and labelling.

Brand Story

For our coconut business, the story behind the brand and our ongoing Cause was why our products existed. It was so important that I made sure our story was on every product label we produced. It was not just a fabricated marketing spiel; it was a true story with real people, family members and a shared history. Our consumers became so supportive of our efforts.

While most companies do not have such a history behind them, they still have a story. It is crucial to engage with your customers, put a human side to your business and help them understand everything your brand stands for.

Brand Colour

When I created the *Banaban* brand, the colour was one of the most critical aspects of overall brand development. Even though we were initially selling only online and were not interested in retail displays, online selling is based on visual appearance. One of the most important ways to stand out online is by using colour. Over the years, I had different graphic artists who wanted to change or soften our blue "beach" branding, but it was not negotiable. Our products "popped" off the screen. This really assisted in helping our brand attain number one status and hold that over the next fourteen years, as competition grew.

In fact, quite a few other brands tried to copy and emulate our colours and design. We were able to hold our own with a dedicated approach to only implement minimum changes over the years to retain our brand identity. The colour was so important to our overall branding that I even went to the extent of having all our plastic product lids made in the matching blue colour. It assisted in making our products stand out more, and much harder to copy our branding.

Brand Packaging

The best advice I can give regarding developing strong branding throughout your packaging is to stay consistent. Do not change your brand design or colour, even if you need to develop various forms of packaging. They should all retain a familiar theme and colour from bottles, jars, pouches, packets, boxes, and cartons. The aim is brand recognition.

Whatever products you develop, your customers need to know immediately that it is your brand. It can sometimes prove quite a challenge, especially when you move from round jars to flat-pack packaging. It is easy to get carried away with a new product launch and overlook the most essential aspect: consistent branding. Your customers must be confident that it is your brand, not another company trying to imitate you.

Brand Messaging

I cannot emphasise enough how important it is to carry your branding through to your everyday business processes and procedures. Of course, this is not always easy if your company sells multiple brands. In my case, our company

Nature Pacific represented natural Pacific Island products, and our key brand was *Banaban*. Everything was branded: our stationery, websites, social media pages, uniforms, factory design, vehicles and signage.

From our notepads to our business cards or our vehicles travelling along the highway, they all carried the same message and strong branding.

While I have highlighted product brand development, many of the same principles can be utilised for personal brand development and the services you provide.

Just as I did in the early 1990s when I first started to publicise the plight of the Banabans; I marketed them just like I would any product brand.

LIFE LESSON: *Your branding message has to be strong and consistent from a simple business card right through to your products on the shelves!*

Online to Retail to Wholesale to Bulk

From 2008, the rate of our company's growth was impressive. Our coconut oil production was now back in full swing, and the cash was flowing in from our online sales.

It gave us the cash flow we needed to hire two more staff, buy some much-needed equipment on rent-to-buy schemes and fund full containers of oil every six weeks for around US$80,000 at a time. A fantastic feat after juggling such limited supply over the past twelve months.

Just as Con predicted, we were hitting critical mass. What was also an exciting aspect at this time was the fact that up until this period, we had built our whole business on online retail sales.

We had enquiries coming in daily from national health food chains, national distributors, wholesale stores and overseas.

Other than our website and eBay listings, we had never put a cent into marketing. I was also using Alibaba's free listings to boost our global reach. Because we entered the eCommerce market in 2004, we were fortunate our listings appeared globally via Google and other search engines. Our products and the strong Island blue branding were popping up on computer screens everywhere.

When we first began the business in the Garage of Dreams with limited supply, I was more concerned about how I would market larger quantities.

We now had the Fijian farm finally ramped up with production and demand for our products increasing every day; I had a new challenge. How to service the demand?

When we started the business online, I had no idea of the traditional and accepted way to market products through national or state distributors. I didn't understand the full extent of their services to carry your product range and have a sales team market your products through their various sales channels.

I soon found out that distributors believed the new age of selling online was a passing phase. They considered companies like ours as smaller operators and not a serious threat to their extensive distribution networks.

I had discussions with various Queensland distributors, who all informed me that they wanted to sell our brand.

The main proviso was that we would have to stop selling online and give them exclusive rights to market our brand.

This conventional or the perceived "right way" of marketing and distributing products was totally at odds with what I had started online.

There were other aspects of this model that I was not keen on:
- The distributor dealt directly with the wholesalers and customers.
- The customer base was the distributors' property, and we would have no direct relationship with our customers.
- We would have to supply our products at wholesale pricing of around 50% off our current retail, and a further 30% would be allocated to the distributor.
- Our daily cash flow would have to change to 30-day accounts, and we would be funding initial stock for a 60-day turnaround.
- Additional marketing campaigns would mean offering further discounts or paying for in-store promotions.

I knew we had a product that people liked and wanted. The results and potential we had online was already evident. I based my confidence on facts. We were getting, on average, a 27% new customer growth rate daily, and we had around a 30% repeat customer rate.

10. Creating a separate organic range was vital for the new mainstream distribution sales channel.

Our regular customer base was growing rapidly. So why did we have to be like everyone else? With over 100% profit margin on our online sales, we could offer generous bulk discounts.

Selling directly to our consumers provided valuable feedback. It gave us control over our supply and enabled us to juggle our sales to meet demand. It also assisted us to slow sales down if there were delays with our supply from Fiji.

At that stage of our company's development, I politely declined the state-wide distribution offers. However, I agreed to supply our brand to a major health store chain with Australian-wide distribution. They didn't insist on exclusivity or require us to cease our online sales.

We were only a few years into the new Factory of Dreams. We had 260 square metres of floor space bulging at the seams with stock, packaging, and raw material. Ken was working night shifts in production to keep up with the orders.

More importantly, our new health store chain kicked in after the initial sixty-day turnaround period. After four months, our products were starting to fly off the health food shelves.

This new distribution channel proved successful, and before we knew it, they were placing orders for $100,000 worth of stock every month. I believed we had found a good sales balance that was working well for us.

The health food chain gave us Australia-wide retail coverage. At the same time, our online sales had us supplying our products to the remotest communities.

Australia's mining boom was in progress, and we soon found demand for our products in some of the remotest mining towns. Who would have thought that these communities could provide us with some of our best sales channels?

The strength of "word of mouth" marketing was so evident in these isolated regions. In some towns, we found one of the townsfolk would take orders, and we would ship to one central location.

Australia Post came to the fore in these remote regions, and customers had no objections to expensive freight bills.

Looking back at these developments and the network we were building with people all over the country, was one of my happiest and most gratifying achievements. We even had friends tell us they couldn't believe it when they found a full range of our products sitting in an outback trading store in the Northern Territory. Places that were so remote and yet our products were there, and the locals loved them.

More importantly, our *Banabans - the Forgotten People of the Pacific* brochures were included with every order and were travelling far and wide. Our important *Banaban* message linked to our Banaban community website was carried on every product we sold.

The next development was to supply bulk oil mainly for manufacturers, so we created a 20-litre pail. The pails worked within the local 24-kilogram shipping limit, and we soon developed a whole new bulk customer base.

This also led to people buying our bulk oil and reselling it under different brand names.

However, at this stage, our *Banaban* branding with Fijian produced oil was strong. The resellers did not impact on our regular sales and only expanded our market share further.

We found our bulk oil going mainly into new markets for food and body product manufacturing and other interesting markets such as racehorse, greyhound breeders, stud cattle breeders, and pet food manufacturers.

These markets only reinforced the claims we were touting about the excellent benefits of coconut oil.

We covered all three marketing areas: online retail, wholesale health store distribution and bulk to other manufacturers and resellers.

 **LIFE LESSON:** *Innovation and leadership are not about following what everyone else is doing but trailblazing your own path.*

Going Global

For those wanting to expand your product sales and venture into the rest of the world, I hope my overview with tips and advice will assist you in your endeavours. More importantly, I hope it will prevent you from making some of the costly mistakes I made over the years. Exporting and selling your products overseas is quite a complex process and, in some cases, not for the faint-hearted.

11. The family team outside the Factory of Dreams No.1 and No 2 Gold Coast.

My aim here is to help provide a short summary of what I discovered about going global. It was a part of our business that I became passionate about.

All the wonderful experiences promoting the Banaban Cause and trading online had given me a great appreciation of other cultures and foreign economies, markets and business practices.

The internet revolution opened doors globally, and I formed so many friendships and embraced learning about how people in different countries viewed the world. Regardless of where we all came from, I found the overall appreciation of our shared humanity carried forward into the business world.

General hints

Every country has its own import laws, and I need to emphasise that these regulatory requirements can change. You need to keep updated of these changes that can significantly affect your overseas sales channels.

The Australian Trade and Investment Commission (Austrade) can provide you with invaluable background Country information and provide you with various export services. One of their services is financial assistance through its Export Market Development Grants (EMDG) programme.

When it comes to actual funding your products to expand overseas, the Australian government can assist. They can provide you with unsecured loans, longer-term loans, bonds and buyer finance through Export Finance Australia (formerly known as EFIC).

While markets and sales channels may appear similar in other countries to what we have in Australia, I had to dedicate time to research and understand each country's markets, customer expectations and overall cultural customs.

These are the three different marketing channels that we worked with:
- Online Sales
- Overseas Distributors
- Bulk Export Shipments.

They all have different requirements. I have listed some key points to consider when entering this market.

Remember, this advice is based on my experiences – we were dealing in organic and non-organic coconut food-grade oil, natural body, hair, and pet products for these markets.

Online Sales – Shipping from Australia

If you are thinking about setting up different pricing for each country, many of the eCommerce sites available offer the ability to sell in multiple currencies. Alternatively, some companies set up dedicated websites for each country. Some major trading sites like Amazon have installed geo-blocking and redirect sellers and buyers back to the country they reside in.

We traded on our Australian website and utilised eBay with international access to sell mainly overseas. Some of the key points to consider:

Pricing currency

Many overseas sites trade in US dollars (USD). If using Australian dollars, I highly recommend adding multiple currencies to your website. You will be amazed at how many overseas customers will abandon sales at checkout when they find only Australian dollars, not other currency options.

Packaging

Needs to be robust, clean, and strong enough to ensure your goods arrive in perfect condition.

Weight and size limits

Small online parcel sales are usually limited to between 20-22 kg. Overall, parcel dimension limits can vary depending on the international shipping provider you use.

Export paperwork

My best advice is to provide as much information and paperwork with your goods to assist in clearing customs. Simple steps such as detailed description, HS (Harmonised System) tariff code and enclose a commercial invoice.

LIFE LESSON: *Just because your brand and marketing are very successful in Australia, do not assume it will work the same in other countries.*

Setting Up Global Distributors

Setting up overseas distributors requires a different approach and is an entirely different level of exporting. The main difference is that your distributor represents your brand and all your brand stands for.

I found some fantastic distributors, or should I say they found me. In the majority of cases, while they all came with their various levels of business acumen, experience, and expertise, most had no in-depth knowledge of virgin coconut oil. The saying in business: "no one knows or understands your products like you do" is a valid statement.

It is up to you to educate your distributors about your products' benefits or why they should invest time and money to promote and sell your products for you. This is where you need to focus on your communication and relationship with your distributors; to share your vision and brand mission, and above all, your overall expectations. In the end, your overseas distributor will be the face and representative of your brand in their country.

The key aim is for them to share as much of your passion as possible. Exporting branded and packaged products is a totally different ball game from selling your products online. It is also very different from exporting bulk raw materials.

There are some key factors when setting up International Distributorships.

International Distribution Agreement

Once you decide to go down this track, you need to have a Distribution Agreement drawn up; an agreement that can easily be edited to suit different countries, locations and currencies.

I had people tell me that you should not give sole distribution rights to an entire country. I decided this was not the way I wanted to go. Instead, I wanted to build our overseas network based on relationships. I also wanted to give our distributors time to prove themselves and build our brand over a set period based on targets.

I based targets on a dollar value, not a product volume figure. This allowed our distributors to test the market to see what products would sell in their country. Of course, you can set your targets to suit your own business and requirements.

I found it best to work out targets based on the first order to allow them to set up their sales channels and a second order to be placed around a three- to six-month timeframe. By the end of the first twelve months, we would expect at least a 10% increase in their orders. Over the next three years, the sales volumes should have increased.

From my experience, you can quickly tell within the first few orders if your distributor will work out. Targets can also give you an easy "out" of your agreement if things are not working out as planned. Let's face it, your distributor also does not want to be stuck with products he cannot sell. So, targets can be a good option for both parties.

Over the years, I found the people who wanted to tie us up with sole distribution fell over quickly when I told them they would have to sign a commitment to our targets.

12. Stacey and Ken showcasing their products as part of the Pacific Island stand at FoodEx trade exhibition in Tokyo, Japan 2012.

At this point in your negotiations, you offer them a trial shipment first to see how they go. You will soon see if your overseas buyer is serious.

Countries have different requirements regarding importing and selling of imported finished goods. This can cause a lot of headaches, especially when you are selling organic products and food.

My best advice for setting up export markets is to be prepared for the extra time and effort you must put into it. It can be well worth it, but, in most cases, it is a slow slog to get it up and running, very different to your usual dealings on a local level.

Labelling

Once you are exporting finished or packed goods for resale, labelling can be an issue. You need to be guided by your distributor, who should be fully aware of what is required for their country. It is best to keep your labelling as simple as possible.

Over the years, like many other Australian manufacturers, I believed that Australia's strict food laws would hold us in good stead when exporting, especially when some countries have much looser regulations in this regard. This was a total misconception, and I was shocked to find that even Australia's highly respected Therapeutic Good Administration in some countries meant nothing at all.

If you would like to export organic products to European Union (EU) countries, it is compulsory to have the appropriate electronic COI certificate (Certificate of Inspection). This certificate is administered through

TRACES (Trade Control and Export System). This means, whatever organic body you have your products certified under in Australia must be recognised and part of the TRACES system. The days of shipping your organic goods with just the appropriate manual paperwork and certificates are well and truly over. My experience of this was only with EU countries.

Please be warned! Your shipment will be rejected at the port of entry if your organic goods are not registered under the TRACES system, which is a huge concern for any exporter.

Depending on your export shipments size, you may need to look at new labelling or new packaging. Alternatively, will the country in question permit over-labelling? If they do, will your distributor do this on their end, or expect you to do this before the goods leave?

It can be an expensive exercise in Australia with our labour costs and is not as simple as it sounds. Details regarding labelling need to be sorted out before you quote pricing or sign any distribution deals. With all the different types of packaging you are using, this can add additional expense and more resources labour wise needed for your manufacturing schedules.

In the end, you need to do your homework, do a full assessment of the pros and cons, and see if the deal is worth pursuing. Could your company's funds, time and efforts be better utilised elsewhere?

From my experience, emerging markets were a good money-spinner, especially for exporting bulk raw material. Going global was part of our broader mission to spread the story and history of the Banabans far and wide. Just like our brand in Australia, all our overseas products carried our Banaban story, and this aspect of our negotiations was non-negotiable.

Export Paperwork

Your paperwork is critical when exporting. It can seem quite overwhelming, but once you take the time to put together the necessary documents, it can be well worth the effort. My best advice is to keep your export documentation well-organised to ensure smooth transactions, avoid any problems clearing your shipments, show your overseas buyers your level of professionalism and build confidence.

You need to think about your export paperwork the same as you would a legal contract. A document that facilitates payments to be made, that gets through all the regulatory compliance for that country, evaluates customs duty and taxes, and sets up traceability for food and body products.

I highly recommend you create an Export Checklist of all the documents you require for each shipment. A checklist will ensure that documents are not missed and help avoid costly mistakes, delays, or clearance problems.

Currency

Most countries specify payment for their export products in US dollars. It is the global trading currency. However, sometimes when you are manufacturing products in Australia and quoting and selling in a foreign currency, prices can fluctuate greatly. It is essential to know your bottom line and profit levels. I can recall two episodes when the Australian dollar reached near parity to the US dollar.

So, one of the essential things for me was to set up a US bank account.

Initially, I bought all our raw materials in US dollars, and I started each day checking out the daily exchange rates. I also became quite good at trading US dollars on the Foreign Exchange Market (also known as forex, FX or currency market). My FX broker became an important person in my team.

In past years it was not as easy to set up a US account from Australia, as it is today. One of the major decisions I made was negotiating a reasonable Australian dollar buying rate with many of my overseas suppliers, wherever possible.

I suggest, for anyone starting out in the export market, do your homework. Make your price lists in the different currencies you trade in and know your costs. Leave enough margin as a play or fudge factor to make sure you will make your margins regardless of exchange rate fluctuations. View your exchange rate variation as a bonus, not a loss.

When the Australian dollar drops, it is music to an exporter's ears. However, if you import raw materials and packaging, it also means increased costs. When the Australian dollar is down, some Asian and EU countries prefer to trade in Australian dollars. In contrast, US customers are only interested in dealing in their currency.

A quick note for anyone who is importing from manufacturers in China, they only want to trade in US dollars. Over the years, I could never change any of the China packaging suppliers to work with us in Australian dollars. I found there were a lot of assumptions, or urban myths, regarding the Australian export market.

Myth 1

Overseas importers were prepared to pay more for Australian-made products. I never found this to be the case. In fact, the export trade market is highly competitive and challenging.

Myth 2

Australian manufacturers insist that they make a quality product, so their products should attract premium pricing for export markets. Now in the age of global eCommerce, it does not take long for your overseas customers to see what you are charging in your country. They can also find out what other suppliers are paying and charging globally.

Myth 3

There are software programs that will give you the names, pricing and even the profit margin of traders selling on major sites like Amazon. So, unless your product is a one-off and no one else globally is making it, it will come down to your brand name and global reach marketing-wise. Above all, you must have realistic expectations. 'I want the best quality for the lowest price!' I cannot tell you how many times I heard the same statement during my supply negotiations.

Payment terms

This is another critical aspect that can also tie in with the Incoterms (International Commercial Terms) during your negotiations. I don't know how this policy got so entrenched in my head, but no orders left our factory unless they were paid for when exporting. Many overseas customers asked me for my trading terms over the years, and I replied, 'goods are shipped as soon as payment is received.' Some overseas suppliers will ask for a 50% deposit upfront at the time of order and balance at the time of dispatch. I never asked my customers for deposits when placing an order unless I thought my trade enquiry was coming from a "time-waster".

Scams are also becoming more common, and there are some tips for identifying genuine export enquiries from the time-wasters. If the customer starts talking about placing large orders and does not ask to negotiate on the pricing or ask for product samples first, they are scammers. The minute they add the words, "will you accept credit card payment?", they are guaranteed scammers. Don't waste your time with a reply but make sure you block the sender and delete their email.

If you are asked for your price list and export paperwork, do not give out any information. Make sure you find out first who you are dealing with. They should provide you with the name of their company, contact details, and which country they are contacting you from.

Confirm they are a legitimate buyer and not a competitor solely trying to garner all your sales information. Do your homework and verify prospective customers before handing out your pricing, product specifications, certificates etc. Remember, it takes nothing to photoshop your certificates using your official paperwork or hard-earned licences and certifications, and misuse them.

This is the main reason I never displayed our various trade certificates online to the public, which is a common practice on Chinese manufacturers websites.

Be careful of prospective international distributors who promise the world. They usually don't deliver. As the old sayings go, "talk is cheap", and "actions speak louder than words"; so true. The people who ask the right questions are the people you want to talk to.

I always found that the people I exported to wanted to know about us, and in turn, we wanted to know all about them. In the end, setting up overseas distributors is all about a mutually beneficial arrangement for both parties. These are the people you want to work with.

I maintained stringent payment policies when it came to export sales. I worked on payment via telegraphic transfer on the sight of documents. This was usually based on FOB (Freight on Board) payments. There's more information on the various Incoterms and what they mean below.

Please make sure you add, via sea freight (port name), or via airfreight (airport name), on your paperwork. This detail needs to be stated, or thousands of dollars can be added to the shipping costs. There needs to be a clear understanding of how the goods will be sent and paid for. These details are relevant to your overall quotation or negotiations.

So why did I prefer my overseas customers to pay via telegraphic transfer (TT) instead of a credit card? When you receive a TT, the money arrives in your bank account just like cash. The payment cannot be reversed or challenged, as it can be on a credit card or via PayPal. While these two payment options are the norm for online payments, they are not acceptable for large shipments reaching six-figure amounts.

There is a lot of money at stake at this level of export, and I had the mindset that these large export shipments could turn you rich overnight and send you broke overnight.

These are other terms of payment that I have used.

Letters of Credit (LOC)

A letter issued by a bank to another bank (especially one in a different country) guaranteeing payments made to a specified person under specified conditions.

Irrevocable Letter of Credit (ILOC)

I only used this payment for our Spanish distributor, which I found stressful. What does it mean by irrevocable? The letter of credit cannot be modified unless all parties agree to the modifications.

Sounds simple enough but beware of what is written into the ILOC. In my case, it was the lead time. I was given a large export order with a deadline date to dispatch. If we had not met the deadline, the order and payment could have been null and void.

You need to be aware that every word written in the ILOC cannot be changed, and you need to meet every detail in the ILOC to release your payment. Because it is a bank-to-bank transaction, they are pedantic over the document's wording and details. I had to engage the person in our bank that deals with LOCs, and she went through the documentation with a fine-tooth comb.

Dealing with a Spanish bank and documentation also proved a nightmare, and we had to negotiate on specific details on the document; otherwise, the payment would be in jeopardy. Meanwhile, while all this was going on, the shipment had already been dispatched. With a six-figure amount at stake, the container of goods was already on the water to ensure it met the deadline stated in the ILOC.

My best advice on this topic is, if your customer wants to pay via an Irrevocable Letter of Credit, please contact your bank. Make sure you talk with the person in charge of this area of payments and follow their advice.

When trading in large amounts, these two different types of Letter of Credit allow the customer to use the bank's money while shipments are on long sea journeys.

Trade Finance

What is trade finance, and how can it affect your export orders? Trade finance provides the exporter with advance funding based on a trade purchase order, while an importer might use trade finance to fund the cost of bringing in overseas goods to fulfil the trade order.

So, in simple terms, it means that you can use a third-party company (and there are a few different companies who offer this service, including the Australian Government's AUSTRADE), who will finance your overseas orders, when based on an official purchase order.

You pay them a percentage of the money you need to fill or make the order, and they carry the debt until the payment is received. It will all depend on the negotiated terms of the contract or order.

I only ever used Trade Finance for my import shipments, not my export shipments. However, it can be an effective way to fund your export shipments. In my Spanish shipment case, I had to supply a full 40-foot container of finished products that had to be manufactured with Spanish translated labels, which meant considerable cost and time were involved in this order.

It also meant that we could not fill the order with existing stock in our warehouse, and new stock had to be specially made. This is where the risk factor starts to weigh heavily and should only be done for large orders. In the case of other smaller distributors, over-labelling (if it is legally accepted in their countries) with different language inscriptions is far easier.

When dealing with Trade Finance, it is common for the export paperwork to be assigned to the third-party company (the Funder) instead of the customer you are dealing with.

Incoterms

This is a crucial aspect of your export quotations and documentation. Incoterms tie in with your payment terms, as stated above. There are many different terms, but I am only listing the ones I commonly used:

- EXW, Ex Works. The buyer takes possession and responsibility for the goods as soon as they are picked up from your warehouse.
- FOB, Free on Board. The seller pays all charges to load the goods onto the vessel, and the buyer takes on all costs from this point.
- FCA, Free Carrier. The seller delivers the goods at their expense to a shipping agent stipulated by the buyer, and the buyer takes over all charges from this point.

- CNF, Cost and Freight. The seller includes all the charges involved in getting the goods to the buyer's designated port or airport in their country.
- CIF, Cost Insurance and Freight. Same as CNF but includes the cost of insuring the shipment.

Shipping Agents

If you are importing and exporting, one of your key decisions is finding the right shipping agent to handle all your shipments. I have had many agents over the years, and some have been an absolute disaster who wasted so much money and provided minimal service.

If you are importing food, please get hold of the Australia New Zealand Food Standards Code. The code will give you a full understanding of your product and whether it will incur duty or GST on entry into Australia. It can also help you choose the HS code (Harmonised Commodity Description and Coding System) to use for your raw material or finished products.

This is information your shipping agent should know. However, understanding how my raw materials were manufactured greatly helped me argue my case with Australian customs when clearing or shipping goods. Additional duties and taxes can add unwarranted charges.

I discovered many shipping agents do not know your products like you do or understand how your products are made. These simple mistakes can quickly add up. I also suggest that when you start shipping you double-check every entry on your invoice. Ensure your agents provide an itemised invoice, so each charge additional to the freight is listed.

Charges and foreign currency conversion on US dollar charged freight from the shipping companies can vary greatly. When looking for a good shipping agent, you need to find the one that best suits your type of products and who does not overcharge you with additional or loaded charges. You also need to be assured that they will be available to assist you when problems with your shipments arise.

For example, I had two containers of food products leave Sri Lanka at different times, months before the busy Christmas period. They both ended up transshipping out of Singapore, and due to the busy shipping schedules, they arrived together on the same ship on the Boxing Day holiday. It was a nightmare as both shipments had to be paid for on arrival before they could be cleared. Our factory was closed, no banks were open, and shipping agents were on holiday.

The following year, this exact situation happened again and caused unbelievable stress. It put a real damper on my family's Christmas celebrations.

Usually, shipping companies allow between five to seven free days for the container to be cleared through customs and quarantine, unpacked, and returned. Once you go past this timeframe, a demurrage fee is charged at a daily rate. If your goods are held in storage, you can face storage fees of over $200 per day.

Over the years, I have spent and lost thousands of dollars on shipping agents and faced many issues. I finally employed a shipping agent on my staff; her knowledge was invaluable and saved us on average around an additional $1,000 per shipment.

If importing and exporting is a significant part of your business, I can highly recommend having a person with these skills on staff. It will not only save you money but take so much stress out of your export shipments and give you access to many different countries.

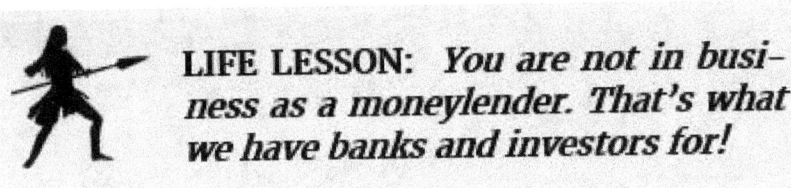

LIFE LESSON: *You are not in business as a moneylender. That's what we have banks and investors for!*

Full Containers vs Less Container Load

I want to shed some insight into the topic of when it becomes viable to import or export full containers (FCL) of goods as distinct from a less container load container (LCL). But first, an LCL is when we don't have enough goods to fill a container. Your shipping agent will organise to consolidate your shipment with others to share space and share the costs.

If your shipment goes above fifteen cubic metres, it becomes far more viable to ship via a container even if it remains half empty. When trying to decide between a full container or LCL, you need to study your freight quotation.

Do not just focus on the freight component but look at all the additional charges. This includes the costs for LCLs to be moved to a warehouse where the goods can be inspected by Customs, unpacked and repacked.

Depending on the country we shipped to, we would use international couriers for shipments under 100 kilograms.

13. Our Banaban Mogolia distributors at the first natural products trade show held in the country.

While the costs might seem expensive, they offer door-to-door delivery and handle all the customs duties where applicable. If they were placing smaller orders, I'd ask an overseas customer if they had their own shipping accounts.

Airfreight can also be another option for smaller shipments, and to remote-destination countries. I often used air freight to ship goods up to 100-kilograms to South Korea. I had a client in Finland who chose to send their one, 200-litre tote of coconut oil via airfreight. The shipment would have taken months to get there via sea freight.

When we imported all our artefacts from Papua New Guinea, we used an air container that held around half a tonne. We packed and cleared it with PNG Customs ourselves at Port Moresby airport and sealed it before we flew back in time, before it arrived.

Air container costs will vary depending on the airline and the freight space available. If not booking a full air container, make sure you use much lighter plastic pallets to reduce the overall weight.

LIFE LESSON: *When dealing with overseas customers asking for trading terms, remember it is near impossible to chase money owing in overseas countries.*

Supply Chain Management/Logistics

Supply chain management brings together multiple processes to achieve a competitive advantage. Whereas logistics refers to the movement, storage, and flow of goods, services, and information within the overall supply chain. So why is this important for exporters?

In our case, we were manufacturers who brought in raw materials and sold them as bulk raw materials or turned them into finished goods under Australian regulatory standards. Our company's growth would not have happened without a strong emphasis on our supply chain management and our logistic strategies for the best way to get our goods to our customers.

We had our own warehouse facility and two different packaging areas. One exclusively targeted online orders, with couriers coming in and out to pick up goods four times a day. The other area was for packing bulk orders onto pallets for pick-up by different freight companies. When shipping export orders, various factors came into the packaging and how the orders were freighted out.

Your packaging should be new, and each carton clearly marked with the contents. Only new or good quality ISPM 15 (international approved heat-treated) stamped wooden pallets should be used for export. If not, your shipment can be rejected at the destination country over phytosanitary and quarantine controls.

When shipping full containers, your agent will arrange for an empty container to be dropped at your premises, and you pack it yourself. Again, you should have clear instructions from your buyer on whether their goods are to be on pallets or loosely packed.

Why is this important? It will depend on how your buyer is clearing goods at their end. Are they going to be unpacked at the wharf and transshipped by road to another location? Will they be stored at a logistic warehouse, or will they go directly to the buyer's facility for unpacking?

The cost can quickly mount if you have to pay to hand unpack a container. On the other hand, you can loose-load your goods into a container instead of palletised stock.

Make sure you are fully aware of your buyer's requirements. It won't get you off to a good start if you don't follow your buyer's instructions. Ensure you have factored these details and any additional costs in at the earlier stage of your negotiations.

Fulfilment Centres/Third Party Logistics (3PL)

Since I began selling online in the early 1990s, eCommerce has greatly evolved and expanded. With these new developments, there is much more global reach and international markets available for our products. Fulfilment centres or 3PLs are third party logistic company providers that specialise in order fulfilment.

This entails you sending your stock to the provider's warehouse centre. Depending on your contractual agreement with them, they can handle the complete process from the point-of-sale enquiries to delivering your product to your customers.

These services are now available in Australia via companies such as Amazon, Invenco, StarTrack, PikPak, NPFulfillment, Coghlan, Pack & Send, to name a few. Amazon operates fulfilment centres in the United States, Canada, Mexico, Brazil, the United Kingdom, France, Germany, Italy, Spain, Czech Republic, Poland, Slovakia, Japan, and India.

There are so many international fulfilment companies now available. You need to do your research to find the one that best suits your export markets and the products you sell.

Warehouse vs Distribution Centre

A distribution centre can handle everything from shipping to selling your goods; unlike fulfilment centres, they do not ship to retailers or individuals. A distribution centre is ideal if you have an agent to represent you in a different country.

The distribution centre can also act as a warehouse to store your goods but be more suitable for short-term storage. A warehouse, on the other hand, usually stores your bulk goods for more extended periods. They do not have the same level of activity as that found in a distribution centre.

With all these logistic options available, you can crunch the numbers and decide which option best suits your business. In my case, I was seriously considering launching our products on the US market via Amazon Fulfilment. However, when I broke down the costs, the level of competition on the market, and the fact I would need to invest about $42,000 worth of stock and new labelling, I believed the level of inventory required could be better utilised in other markets.

Just remember that the longer your goods sit in overseas distribution, fulfilment centres or 3PLs, the more your costs increase. You need to be confident that stock will move quickly, that the fees charged are well covered, and your profits make it worth your while.

Exporting Bulk Shipments

Just like the other export markets I have described, bulk shipments require the same amount of export paperwork although a slightly different approach.

Bulk shipments usually refer to 20 or 40-foot containers that generally get packed by your staff at your facility. Therefore, it is important to think about how the goods will travel while at sea. How will they be unpacked at the destination port? Or will they be transported via truck over long distances to their final destination?

Remember that the ocean can provide a rough ride for your container, and in really bad weather, containers can be lost overboard. Also, consider that while at sea, your stock can be subjected to extreme temperatures.

If you sell to the northern hemisphere, your goods will cross through the hot tropics and arrive in the middle of a northern winter. Can your goods survive these conditions in a regular container, or do you need to book a temperature-controlled reefer container?

There are some key points to consider.

Be confident your bulk packaging will meet your buyer's requirements and meet the phytosanitary regulations (relating to plant-based packaging or products) to your destination country?

Ensure your bulk packaging or cartons have labels relating to contents and match your export documentation's product descriptions.

If using cardboard packaging, it should be new and clean. It should be kept dry and not packed out in the open in wet weather conditions. (See more information under Canada below).

Your shipping agent may require an MSDS (a Safety Data Sheet). This document goes into the ship's manifest. It ensures the captain is aware of any safety concerns (chemical, flammable) in your container.

When packing on pallets, ensure they are export grade ISPM15 certified in good condition and free of dirt. Will the destination country even accept wooden export pallets; Brazil does not allow timber pallets and has stringent regulations in this regard?

When packing your container, please ensure you brace the goods inside to avoid any movement during transit. Just remember, your container could end up on the top of a stack on the deck of a huge cargo ship that will be rolling all over the place. Your goods could end up significantly damaged during the time at sea.

Be aware of issues that can arise using fillers for packing in your containers. Due to the long sea journey and high humidity, water-soluble bio-fill void packing can collapse, and goods can suffer damage in transit.

If you use other types of void filling, packing fibre or internal wrapping in your cartons, will they comply with the country's Phytosanitary regulations? Will they also stand up to the high humidity during shipping?

Just like ensuring your goods and outer packaging are clean, you must ensure that your container's floor has been swept and cleaned of debris or food spills. If your container has been packed sitting in mud or arrives with dirt or other debris on the outside, it could be deemed a bio-risk, and your container could require a container wash at the destination port.

When dealing with these much larger bulk shipments, we are in an area where large amounts of money are at risk. Usually, you are working on lower margins, and profits based on volume at this level.

The cost to fulfil these large shipments can be a significant issue, and Trade Finance or an Angel Investor could be essential to take you to this next step. I was fortunate to fund a lot of our company's growth through these types of export sales.

I loved the export and import part of our business. I think of the earlier years working with Alberto, exporting his powders. His wealth of experience in the field gave me a head start in our coconut oil business.

I had also learnt a few lessons earlier on during the initial online global sales, via eBay, of our tribal artefacts to some of the remotest places in the world. All these experiences assisted me in the early days of the emerging global eCommerce revolution.

14. The question Stacey is often asked, how they became one of the Top 101 International Sellers with Alibaba, China?

CHAPTER 6

THE BIG QUESTION – CHINA?

One of the questions I am frequently asked is how we were awarded the "Top 101 International Seller" in 2016? I also often get asked about our collaboration with Alibaba in China.

Alibaba China

My connection to Alibaba goes back to before the beginning of our coconut business, when I was exporting natural powders globally. This company, which I still own and operate today, commenced in 1999. Ironically, Alibaba also began in April the same year, founded by Jack Ma in Hangzhou, China.

In the early days of the internet, Alibaba was an excellent global trading site with a powerful search engine presence, similar to eBay. It was not targeting eBay's retail customer base but became the international online gateway for the Chinese manufacturing sector.

At this stage of our business, I was not interested in entering the mainland China export market. I was only interested in using Alibaba to list all my bulk Australian-made natural health powders I was marketing and exporting, for Alberto. South Korean and United States pharmaceutical and nutraceutical manufacturers were the main target markets.

In the early years of Alibaba, we were able to place free listings on the site, and my focus was on trading bulk oil globally. Only a few Australian companies were listed on the site initially, but Alibaba's reach was excellent. Enquiries came in from around the world, and I am sure most of my overseas distributors found us through this site. One of the important status levels in Alibaba was to be recognised as a Gold Seller.

This status level was not available to Australian companies in the early stages, but this changed around 2008 when Alibaba decided to target more Australian companies. The fact that Jack Ma had lived and gone to university in Australia had helped that decision.

I originally received a phone call from China from a young man called Daniel, who informed me of the new Gold Seller status. Of course, my initial reaction was "another scam call". However, he had an intimate knowledge of my Alibaba history, and how long I had traded with the company. I must admit that during our various phone conversations, I put him through the wringer.

Daniel always stayed calm and answered all of my concerns. He wanted me to pay an annual US$400.00 fee to upgrade to the Gold status. I asked, 'Why would I spend money when I already have results from your free trading service?' Again, Daniel explained the benefits, and I told him to leave it with me. He came back to advise me they wanted our company onboard, and I was offered a special US$200.00 deal. Due to his persistence and the fact he was so calm and polite, I took up the offer.

Every year from that point on, if I needed something or when my annual subscription was due, Daniel personally phoned me, and our relationship developed from there.

Like all things in business, relationships develop over time and through mutual respect and trust.

About two years before Alibaba was ready to launch in Australia, they had already asked to film a story about our company at our facility. This led to us being awarded the top "101 International Seller" award. I was fortunate to have been flown to Alibaba's headquarters in Hangzhou.

I had a fantastic week with a hundred of the other 101 winners, mostly young Chinese businesspeople, except for three men, two of whom had a furniture manufacturing business in Indonesia, and the other a South Korean businessman.

I found myself with two full-time Chinese entrepreneurs and a fabulous team of young, vibrant Alibaba staff, with a high percentage being women. Daniel, my original contact all the years before, had already left Alibaba by that stage.

I soon found that once staff reached thirty years of age in the corporation, they usually branched out independently. Daniel had done exactly that but still had business connections with Alibaba. It was great when he turned up to meet me while I was there.

By February 2017, Ken and I had the privilege to have another company video produced by Alibaba, featuring at their Australian launch in Melbourne. My experience with Alibaba has always been a positive one and is an excellent example of the strength of building long-term business relationships.

LIFE LESSON: *Some of the best connections for your export markets can be sitting here in your own backyard.*

China Market Challenges

Over the years, the trade opportunities between Australia and China have grown rapidly. Due to our company having such a high profile with Alibaba, people assumed that we were using Alibaba as the gateway for selling our products in China. We were not, but for Australian manufacturers, the possibility of 1.3 billion Chinese consumers loving Australian products outweighs the difficulties of selling into this market.

Chinese are brand driven. Australian baby milk formula and other established brands have mainly been marketed and sold through Australia's daigou networks. The daigou (pronounced dye-go) is an eCommerce sales channel between Chinese professional shoppers in Australia and mainland China customers.

The daigou sellers usually ship their goods through the mail. They have established their own Australian-based freight companies, offering excellent rates to land products direct to consumers or their designated resellers in China. In the past, because of the difficulties Australian companies faced exporting into mainland China, most companies exported to Hong Kong instead and distributed their products from there.

Unlike Australia, Chinese companies need an import licence, with products approved before importation into the country. These permits can take months to get approval. In the case of body products, a bone of contention for Australian manufacturers is that China insists on the products being tested on animals. You usually need to work with a Chinese agent or importer to negotiate all this for you.

I have heard nightmare stories of Australian companies going through these negotiations, which included providing formulas and ingredient lists, then finding after months and even years of negotiations that their products were copied and marketed directly by unscrupulous Chinese companies.

Exporting into China is a revolving door and subject to political change that affects import tariffs, regulations and, in some cases, trade bans. You need to do your research and not assume anything when entering this market. There are many points to consider. Do not assume that because you produce the best quality, Australian-made products, Chinese customers will pay for them. They still want the best quality and the lowest price; it is the reality of the situation.

If you don't quickly file a trademark on your brand name and product in China, someone else will, and you can find your company and brand blocked from trading there.

There are many so-called experts offering services to get your products launched in China; be wary. I suggest paying Austrade to check them out. Spending money to identify legitimate experts is money well spent.

What clinical trials or testing will your products need in the process, for example, baby products? What is involved in getting your product registered to sell in China? How long will it take? If you get a supply contract with China, make sure you will have the raw materials and manufacturing capabilities to fulfil contracts. Can you find the money to fund it all? Do you want to put your company at risk to enter this market?

Make sure your products fit culturally into the Chinese market. Is the brand name translation offensive? Is it a new product? How will they perceive it? Have you carried out extensive market research within the Chinese community in Australia first?

The massive Chinese consumer market is like a pot of gold surrounded by a vault in a heavily armed fortress. It is protected by the Chinese government who implements the laws to protect its consumer markets. If a product does become popular, Chinese investors like to invest in these products to benefit from these lucrative markets.

We hear stories of Australian companies being bought out and the millions involved. These are the success stories for the companies concerned, but there is also another side to the story. Don't just look initially at the money involved, but focus on the products as this is your goal to export success in China.

The first essential step is to build your brand name presence here in Australia with your local Chinese community. The number of Australians in Australia with Chinese ancestry was 1.2 million (2016 census). The number of Australian daigou sellers (Nielsen Report, 2017) was estimated between 100,000 and 200,000.

People were shocked when I told them I had not entered the Chinese market. There are a number of reasons. The Chinese people do not like the taste of coconut oil. They are used to oilseed; cooking oils with peanut oil and vegetable oil being the most popular. I found that the smell of coconut was not considered as pleasant to Chinese people.

It even made some of the consumers reluctant to put it on their skin. We sent a trial shipment of body oils via Hong Kong for Chinese mainland consumers. When they saw the oil had set solid white, they believed it was pig fat.

In Australia, the younger Australian daigou shoppers are more aware of the health benefits and popularity of the products here in Australia. The older generation, especially the major buyers, found it hard to see any health benefits. They considered coconut oil was made in poor Pacific and Asian countries by people who could not afford to buy imported vegetable oils.

I was not interested in selling bulk coconut oil to China for several reasons:

- I could not supply the amount they would need for an ongoing supply contract,
- It would have put our farms under pressure,
- It would have affected our existing supply requirements, including supplying the lowest profit margins to compete in this market. In other words, increased supply with much higher costs and reduced profit margins. All our farms were subject to natural disasters with tropical storms and cyclones. Large supply

contracts can quickly become "null and void" if you cannot meet your supply commitments.

For these reasons, I decided the mainstream export Chinese market was not for us. There were far better markets to be had, especially in countries with emerging market economies.

The World is Waiting

Our products shipped to every corner of the globe with our online sales, from Alaska in the northern hemisphere to the remote Falkland Islands. We worked with distributors and agents, shipping large bulk shipments and thousands of *Banaban* branded finished goods in the following countries: Hong Kong, South Korea, Taiwan, Singapore, Japan, Mongolia, Canada, United States, Germany, Hungary, Poland, Malta, Spain, Serbia, United Kingdom, Finland, New Zealand, Chile, Brazil, and Columbia.

I have only focused on my unique experience with Alibaba and why I was not looking to export bulk to mainland China. I could write a book on my experiences in each one of the countries we exported to. They all have a back story behind them, and they all had different import requirements that provided some of the greatest challenges and rewards.

I loved expanding our brand globally and working with the wonderful people we worked with. I enjoyed every moment of the experience, even when different country regulations and nuances proved challenging.

It was the part of our business I truly relished.

CHAPTER 7

A DREAM INVESTOR WITH NO HIDDEN AGENDA

With talk of expanding into export markets, the big question was how to fund it? We all face this question when our business takes off, and we need to fund stock. We had to fund importing our oil from the farms, then manufacturing and bottling the products before turning them around for sale.

If everything went to schedule, we looked at a three-month turnaround. Of course, selling bulk oil offers a quicker turnaround but also lowers margins. It got to the stage in our business growth that I realised the demand for our bulk oil was on a global scale.

We had new farms in Vanuatu that were able to support our supply chain, while our farm in Fiji had increased production to meet our Australian demands.

The Factory of Dreams was bulging at the seams, and we had already expanded to two more adjoining factories. Our original factory was dedicated to bottling and product manufacturing. It included our main office with a small retail shop and front office. The next-door premises, Factory No. 2, housed our finished products, packaging, and dispatch. Once the second factory was fully stocked and working to capacity, we leased the adjoining premises. This one was used for bulk storage of raw materials, in and out.

Having three factories in the one complex meant we had more car park space. The Factories of Dreams were a hive of activity. Shipping containers were being packed and unpacked in the car parks while the couriers and freight trucks were in and out all day.

With so much expansion, including more monthly overheads, I became an expert juggler. I could buy new equipment and machinery, even our second-hand forklift, on "rent to buy" contracts, which avoided taking much-needed cash out of our cashflow for capital expenses. The seller does not always mention they offer this service until they realise you are a serious buyer. They offer a "rent to buy" contract to get the deal over the line. You will be surprised how many will accommodate you. It just means they break down the final price into a monthly payment, usually over three years, and add a bit of interest. It's easy, and usually it's in the contract terms that the seller retains the equipment's ownership until paid in full.

The next option is financing via the usual banking and finance channels, and the lender holds the security over the equipment until full payment is made. Some equipment can be purchased on full monthly rental terms.

We used this scheme to buy a brand-new forklift for our business. Because the forklift company retained ownership of the machine, they were responsible for regular servicing and maintenance under the terms of the agreement. They had to cover any repairs if required. This type of deal can save a lot of money in costly repairs and servicing down the track, and the rental charges are tax-deductible.

As my expertise in juggling finances increased, I realised there was a lot of bulk business I was missing out on because I just could not fund it. Anyone who has faced the same problems when trying to fund their business growth will know the stress the lack of funding takes on you. It can cripple and limit your business growth.

About seven years into our business, we had finally hit critical mass. My mind was fixated on supply and funding. My brain worked overtime, thinking of all the ways I could get some capital injection to expand into the global bulk trading market.

I kept hearing the words of my first, long-departed Cornish accountant. When I was young, he had been our family accountant, and I had innocently asked for his advice on business partnerships. His reply left an indelible mark on my psyche for the rest of my business career.

'I have not had one partnership work out and very few marriages.'

His words always stayed in the back of my mind, and I knew that looking for a business partner was not for us.

Next, I thought about splitting our business into two separate companies and divisions. The original business would turn into a contract manufacturer responsible for producing our finished products and handle the sales for online, retail and wholesale markets.

The new company would concentrate on handling all the importing and supply of raw materials for the original company and manage all the bulk supply contracts for exporting only.

I put together a business plan with the idea that I'd bring in investors in the import/export division. I put the proposal to some of my good friends in Japan who had already mentioned they would like to invest in our company. While I appreciated their offers, I needed at least a $100,000 injection to really make a difference.

Unfortunately, while my friends owned large companies in Japan, they had no overseas investments. Typical of all things Japanese, I would have to spend months working with their board to explain the investment required. was not your conventional businesswoman, and in fact, I prided myself on doing things – my way. I realised this wouldn't go over well with traditional Japanese board members. I had to come up with another plan.

I seriously considered selling off the contract manufacturing division. Ken and I would retain ownership of the *Banaba* brand. Another option was to licence our brand to a manufacturer.

Manufacturing was where the most significant expense was in our business. But this risked losing control over our product quality and could become a threat to our brand. Our mission was too important to take this risk.

I heard there was a local investment group working out of Bond University and made enquiries. Similar to the television programmes *Shark Tank* and *Dragon's Den*, it would come down to pitching to prospective investors. If investors were interested, they would expect a percentage share of our company and business.

There was no way we were giving anyone a stake in our company, especially for the sake of a $100,000 investment. Our sales and growth were going through the roof. Back to the drawing board …

I was busy thinking about who else I could talk to, and thought, 'why not speak to our mortgage broker who had helped us get finance for our home years earlier?' He had been born in Fiji and came from a prominent Fijian family but had lived in Australia most of his life. He knew where Ken and I had come from and how vital our Banaban mission was. After explaining what I needed and the options I had already looked at, he said he might have a client, a private investor, who might be a perfect fit for us.

Before I knew it, we met Brian, who ended up becoming our dream, or as the business world calls them, an Angel Investor. After our initial discussions with Brian, I came up with a new plan.

I needed a $100,000 investment over a term of about one year. The investment would commence on a three-month term and roll over every month after that, for a total of twelve months. I offered to pay $5,000 in interest for the first three months and $2,500 a month in interest payments for every month after that.

When we reached twelve months, the investment would either be paid in full or renegotiated again for a month-by-month rollover. So technically, my investor was offered around a 27% return on his $100,000 investment.

Everyone thought I had gone mad. Why would I offer to pay so much interest when bank interest was so low in comparison?

Well, how many of you have been knocked back by the bank when you try to raise funds for capital growth? The bank had supported me with an overdraft in line with the amount of money going daily through our account. But banks do not back risk-takers, and they already had our home as security, another major issue that we will discuss later.

Brian, our Dream Investor, liked us and everything our business stood for, and we liked him. He was a retired businessman who knew what it was like to be in a small business, and he believed in me and what I was doing management wise.

Before I knew it, the deal was done. Brian took a lien over our plant and equipment as security, and the contract was signed off via his lawyer. His lawyer charged me $3,500 to set it up. Typically, from my experience with lawyers, this one was no different and overcharged us.

Brian was undoubtedly a Dream Investor. He dropped by each month to check out our figures and see how we were going. He was always encouraging and glad to see we had invested his money in stock.

At this stage, our annual turnover was just over $800,000. With Brian's $100,000 investment, which we had extended to fifteen months, I had already paid him back $30,000 off his principal investment. This automatically reduced our interest repayments, and our turnover jumped by a million dollars to $1.8 million.

While some of my business colleagues could not believe I'd paid back my investor a third in interest, I was happy with the deal. He never interfered in my decisions but believed in what I was doing and supported my decisions

100%. It was great to have him there with his depth of business experience. Even though he had a lien over our business while the loan was in place, he had no share in our company or business. He gave us the flexibility to roll over his money monthly as I paid down the principal amount over the final months.

The $30,000 spent on his interest payment allowed us to more than double our sales within one financial year. Except for our bank overdraft and some "rent to buy" monthly payments, we were free of any other debt and had a full warehouse of stock.

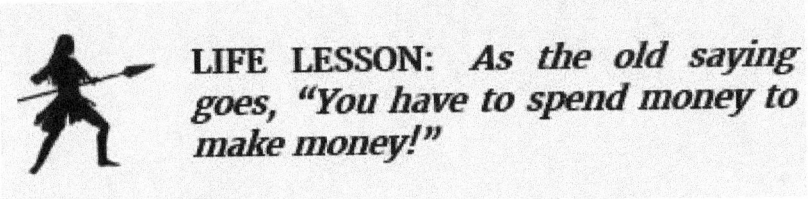
LIFE LESSON: *As the old saying goes, "You have to spend money to make money!"*

Avoiding Punch-ups in the Office

Ahhhhh, the joy of it all ... when you dream of building a business empire that will benefit your whole family and your relatives in Australia and Banaban family back in the villages.

As the business grew, so had our two wayward assistants and their roles within the company. Ken's youngest daughter, Lusinta, spent her teenage years travelling back and forth between Australia and Fiji. She had finally settled in Australia, working with us and we assumed she would spend her time working in production with her father.

15. The Four Factories of Dreams were bulging with stock, thanks to our Angel Investor.

Business, time management, computers and phones were not something she had grown up with. But I knew she was a fast learner, and I had watched how she had embraced the computer when she spent time with us. I also knew the confidence and personality she exuded when she was back home on the Island. It was totally at odds with her time spent working on her own in production.

While I have already mentioned in earlier chapters about not putting people into roles they are not comfortable in, I knew the natural talents Lusinta possessed.

More importantly, I knew she genuinely supported and cared for her father. But the day she arrived back in Australia and walked into the quickly expanding Factories of Dreams, she was shocked to find that her production position was no more.

The look on her face and accompanying deathly silence made it clear she was not happy with my decision. I felt I had just become the wicked stepmother. I needed to utilise her natural skills and personality in our front office; to answer the phone, greet customers and represent the Banaban aspect of our business.

I trusted her to support and protect our backs as more staff began to come on board. Through the non-verbalisation I was receiving, I tapped into her cultural upbringing by calling on her inherited sense of duty. Of course, this also meant working with her other wayward assistant, her younger half-sister, Brynley, who had also been promoted to the other front-office position.

In Island custom, an elder's authority is never questioned or challenged. Island children grow up being the masters of holding their tongues and respecting their elders at all costs. What a great virtue, you are all saying? So different from how we raise our children in Australian society. Our children, in comparison, are spoilt and indulged, and in general want for nothing. What I have always encouraged with my children is to question and hopefully not blindly follow.

I encouraged my son to iron his clothes, and when he complained, I told him that he would thank me one day. I wanted him to marry someone because he loved them and not because he wanted a woman to take care of him. I encouraged my children to become independent, free-spirited adults.

In principle, it may be an idyllic approach. In reality, it can add to noisy debates and challenges, which is totally at odds with the Island principle of keeping your lips well and truly zipped. I hope I have given a clear picture of our basic family dynamics.

While I realise that many companies are not family-run businesses, there are many that are or have started that way. Whatever company or business you operate, personality clashes, office politics, and family dynamics can greatly impact your business.

The more people you employ, the more aspects of their lives you need to manage. Of course, as an older woman in business who had raised three children, my natural instincts kicked in and, dare I say, my mothering skills.

As the Factories of Dreams expanded, I employed more and more extended family members from both sides. Many of them were young and not long out of school, or unskilled, keen, and thankful for the opportunities to earn money and help support their families.

Most of Ken's Banaban extended family members worked with him in production, and he managed them the Island way. At the same time, on my side of the business, the staff fell under my control. This principle worked well for us, but as more outside staff came in, new problems arose.

Islander staff in production found it easier to converse in their language, which led to other staff believing they were being spoken about. A "speak English" policy had to be implemented to stop animosity and tension amongst staff. In some cases, Ken explained, it was hard to try and explain things in English. Still, for workplace safety and the betterment of everyone, there was no argument.

Brynley and Lusinta, the two wayward assistants, had stepped up in their newly appointed front office roles. While the usual family dynamics reared its ugly head on a few occasions, mostly when the work pressure was on, to their credit, they made it work. But with a culturally diversified workforce, other issues soon brought new challenges.

I appointed a local employment agency and was delighted to hear instead of paying for their services, we would be eligible for government funding to hire more staff. What a great idea!

I took up the offer. I didn't understand the more wage relief the government paid, the person had either been unemployed for an extended period or may have other underlying issues.

Due to Australia's strict privacy policy, as the employer we have no access to our employee's information before hiring. While I believe everyone deserves a chance or opportunity to reach their full potential, it also meant we had no understanding of where these new staff members came from or any past challenges they may have faced.

In one extreme example, we had a new warehouse storeman, Jay, who was a fantastic worker. He was a self-starter, happy to work independently, driving the forklift and arranging stock. Even though I had no direct contact with him, I found him polite and respectful. The only negative thing was his choice in loud, heavy metal, headbanging, highly explicit music. Initially, with him working away on his own in Factory No. 3, it was not an issue.

Unfortunately, the situation was soon to change when I employed Don as our new operations manager. He came highly recommended with a background in the packaging and supply industry. Jay and Don both took an instant dislike with each other, and before we knew it, Ken had to stand in between them to prevent an all-out brawl. We soon discovered that our new operations manager was also having issues with other staff.

While Don had come to us with good references, I discovered he hadn't managed a large, diverse team that we had in our company. Instead, he worked with a small sales team that had a very different dynamic.

One day while visiting Factory No. 3, I witnessed an incident between Don and Jay, and I didn't appreciate Don belittling Jay in front of me. It was very apparent Don had a short fuse when it came to managing people. After calling him into my office, I explained that I didn't see his management style as a good fit for our business. It was a relief when we both decided amicably to part ways so he could pursue other career options.

Next, I called Jay, our headbanging storeman, into my office to read him the riot act. He was polite while I calmly explained that I found him to be a good hard worker. As the company owner, I could not allow his unruly behaviour to go on and that no levels of aggression would be tolerated. I further explained I had a duty of care to protect all my staff and provide them with a safe working environment.

I added on a personal level that his behaviour with Don had scared me. He was taken aback and apologised profusely, assuring me it would not happen again. There was more to Jay than I realised. Where had he come from, why had he moved from Sydney to the Gold Coast, why had he been unemployed for so long when he was such a good worker? Why was he becoming a loose cannon ... ex-criminal, drug dealer, you name it?

My mind went into overdrive. Meanwhile, the rumour mill amongst the staff started to rear its ugly head, and I began to hear mention of the word "ice".

After Don's departure, everything started to settle back to normal, and I recruited a woman I had known over the years from the packaging industry. She was strong, assertive, and good at getting problems sorted and the job done. Jean was just the person we needed to fill the operations manager role, but being so direct and a woman brings new challenges.

Jay was starting to exhibit some erratic behaviour. The music was getting louder as he worked even faster and harder. His filters were changing. He was working like a driven man, and now I was hearing swearing and a loud throbbing beat lifting and penetrating the walls of my office. Even our young female staff who were more accustomed to swearing were complaining.

I had put in some research and grasped just how serious ice addiction could be and realised we were entering dangerous territory. Of course, Jean was already on to it. She had no understanding of what had gone on previously. She was handling the situation as subtly as a sledgehammer.

Even Ken, who usually had no problems talking man-to-man to Jay, agreed with me that his position was becoming untenable. The situation had to be managed carefully. Ken and I had come to the same conclusion – he had to go.

Ken and I tried to calmly work out a peaceful strategy for Jay's leaving, Jean marched into my office like a sergeant major and announced that she would gladly go downstairs and give him his marching orders.

While I understood she probably thought Ken and I were weak, I had to explain that this could be a dangerous situation and needed careful handling, not a heavy-handed, in-your-face approach.

Her statement, 'I am afraid of no man,' added to my anxiety. I calmed her down by explaining that we did not want a drug-crazed, disgruntled ex-employee returning, especially if Ken was away overseas. I explained, 'He might want to seek revenge in the middle of a psychosis and want to come back and firebomb our factories.'

She marched back out of the office with strict instructions not to front him. Instead, she called a staff production meeting. True to form, Jay refused to attend. Ken's patience had gone. He was finally done. Jay seemed to become more hostile with Ken, and Ken had no option but to front him head-on. He calmly pointed out to Jay that his tolerance and ability to work with others had deteriorated, and his behaviour had become too volatile.

Ken insisted he could not let things get out of hand and was concerned that both of them could end up in a situation that would not end well. One that they both would regret!

To his credit, Jay agreed with Ken's reasoning, especially when Ken reminded him that his young daughter needed him. The mention of his daughter seemed to bring him back to his senses, and he left the building never to return.

A stressful and highly volatile situation had dissipated, and I felt very relieved. There would be no need to have eyes in the back of my head every time I worked back late on my own or worry about an unhappy ex-employee coming through the door.

With a "three strikes you are out policy", the only way to dismiss staff is to learn and hone your negotiation skills to near-psychology levels. Luckily, Ken had studied and excelled in this field while briefly studying to become a minister at Theology College back in Fiji. The only alternative to removing unsuitable and usually unhappy staff was for them to resign.

We had so many other staff issues over the years, especially when you have beautiful young girls and healthy young men working together. The day the girls complained that one of the older male staff members was seen using his phone to film up the girl's short skirts hit my desk, I gladly passed that issue on to Ken to sort out.

Another episode happened, this time relating to religion. It was one that we never saw coming and one that would become a threat to our business a few years later. But this initial issue began with our efforts to find a new forklift driver and storeman to replace Jay. A young man applied for the position, and I was impressed knowing that he had worked for some time with one of the large local produce stores that happened to be a customer of ours.

I had already realised the candidate came from a middle eastern background. During his interview, he confirmed that he was a committed Muslim and he would need to have certain times of the day available for his devotions. I didn't see this as a problem as he would mostly be working on his own.

We were already a multicultural and diversified family company, so I didn't want to show bias towards other cultures and their beliefs. However, I pointed out that while he would be mostly working on his own, he would have to work with the women and girls in the office and occasionally take instructions from them.

He seemed reserved, but with his religious beliefs, I knew drugs and alcohol would not be an issue. I took him on a tour of the Factories of Dreams. During our walk around, some of our younger female staff members, who just happened to be stunning blondes, had to interrupt us to ask me for instructions.

I noticed his unease when I introduced him to the girls and realised that he might have issues working with women. I left it at that, thought a seven-day trial would do no harm and arranged for him to start the following day. He never showed up, never rang to tell us he wouldn't be coming and was never seen again.

Obviously, his religious beliefs had to come first and working with a female boss, a female sergeant major, and a bevy of attractive young female staff was just not going to work.

With such a growing workforce, I was soon to learn that there were so many other issues that I had never thought of. These included staff having to attend court, and in one case not returning to work, never to be seen again. The young person had asked to take time off to sort out a family issue and never mentioned legal problems.

Once again, due to privacy policies, we as the employers are the last to know, if at all. We usually rely on the staff rumour mill most of the time. I can now say after years of so many different experiences, nothing really shocks or surprises me.

However, there were times when I felt very disappointed. It must be my generation, but I found it hard to believe people could walk out in the middle of their working day, never to be seen again.

I had no idea what was going on personally behind the scenes and issues they might be facing at home. I believed in offering support to all our staff wherever possible. At least a "goodbye", a "farewell", or even, "see you later", or "can you send my pay cheque", was not asking too much.

There was one staffing policy I had in place that I was strict about. If an employee resigned or left the company, unless it was for maternity leave or un-related work issues, they could never come back. I was generous with our staff, and while many of them were young, I had to be strict in this regard. I couldn't allow our company to become a revolving door. But overall, many lovely people worked with us over the years, and I need to mention young Jackson, one of those rare gems.

I had given up on using employment agencies and much preferred to employ people who were recommended, or I knew the companies they had worked for. This gave me a bit of a heads up in having an idea of their working abilities. I put in a lot of extra hours working back late, and occasionally I dropped into the local Subway store on my way home to grab dinner.

Over twelve months, I often ran into a young man called Jackson, whom I assumed was a university student. We usually had a quick conversation as he efficiently made my order. One day he asked where I worked, as I always seemed to work late.

I told him the name of our company down the road, and he mentioned that if I was ever looking for staff, to let him know. I handed him my business card. As the months of the year rolled by, I didn't run into him and assumed he was caught up with the end of year university exams. By the beginning of the following year, we were again looking for more casual staff.

On my next visit to the store, I asked the manager if Jackson, the uni student, was still working there. He laughed and said, 'You mean school student?' I was shocked. Jackson was so mature I couldn't believe he had been a high school student.

I left a message with the manager, and a few weeks later, my young friend phoned me. I immediately offered him a casual position which he was keen to take up as he had just started university. It was a joy to have Jackson working for us. He not only was a great worker but juggled his time studying and university at the same time.

From the first moment I met Jackson, I knew he was special, and my instincts proved correct. The day he finally left us, he had turned twenty-one years of age and had graduated from university with honours. It was a sad and yet happy day to see him moving on and to see the lovely young man he had become. He vowed that one day he would return as CEO to run our company for us.

Today, he has a successful professional career in Sydney.

In a family business, there are more emotions added to the mix. The usual underlying issues common amongst siblings and extended family are heightened, especially if they believe that not all things are equal. Of course, there will always be different leadership levels and management in business that, at times, can be at odds with your usual family dynamics.

In our case, I was the managing director, eventually becoming CEO and making all the management decisions. Ken was the other director, with his responsibilities managing production and his team.

In our business, we had the added factor of being a cross-cultural family. With my two daughters, Riagan and Brynley working in the business, two of my grandchildren eventually helped in school holidays, plus various nieces and nephews.

Initially, my son in law, Adam, was working with Ken in production. At one stage, my son, Aidan, also joined us in the management area for a short stint between his career change. Ken had his youngest daughter Lusinta, who was now married and living permanently in Australia. Eventually, I was able to bring Ken's son Kabuta and daughter-in-law, Tutu and their two children over from Fiji on a 457-work visa to help us.

The production staff was mostly made up of Ken's extended Banaban family, who were now living in Brisbane. The other half of the team were Australian. Ken and I had to bring everyone together into one well-functioning team.

The only way we achieved this was through clearly defining the roles—management and administration under my control and production under Ken. If Ken and I were united, and I didn't interfere with his running of production, everything worked well.

If Ken and I weren't agreeing on something, or I overstepped my authority with his team, Ken would be straight on to me to let me know.

I thought I did a pretty good job of it, especially when internal spats amongst siblings or stepsiblings arose. I on all my mothering skills to be as professional as possible. I told my children that I became their boss the moment they walked through the office door.

One day in the office, my eldest daughter Riagan stated, 'Can you just be my Mum – not my boss?'

Her words hit me to the core!

I automatically answered, 'No, here in the office, I am your boss, not your Mum.'

For us all to survive and for our company to function, I had to be the boss, but Riagan's words kept ringing in my head. Was the business so important that I had lost all sense of being a mum? Was my quest to build a family empire alienating me from my children?

I kept these conflicting emotions tucked away in my head and heart, otherwise I wouldn't have been able to function and make the tough decisions I needed to make daily. While I was trying my best to be there for everyone, I realised that I had to be the boss, manage everything around me, and provide a living and opportunity for us all.

Maybe it still wasn't enough. I also had to remember that my grown children needed me to be in their lives. While I was physically and mentally engaged, I built up my walls guarding my feelings and emotions.

I felt deeply about so many things, but as my life became more enveloped by business, my emotions had become my weakness.

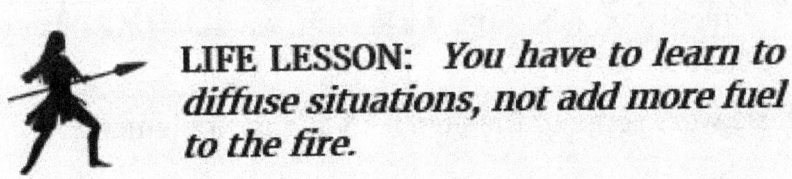

LIFE LESSON: *You have to learn to diffuse situations, not add more fuel to the fire.*

Hang on for the Ride

With significant growth happening in the business, other challenges and stress began to rise. There never seemed to be enough hours in the day, and at times it felt like we were all buckled in for the ride.

While it is exciting to see your hard work starting to gain traction, it is also a critical time in your business. You need to stop somehow, take time, and get control of what is going on around you.

The wheels can fall off if you don't start to build structure. When you start with an idea and making a few products from your garage, your focus is on driving the business forward. Those earlier years of struggle impact your thinking. Thinking about building structure is the last thing on your mind.

It is during this growth period that a lot of companies collapse. It is critical to build structure, and all levels of compliance must be implemented. The days of winging it and just getting by no longer work. You need to stop and focus on all the dreaded boring stuff, the detail. Trust me, you must bite the bullet and create policies on everything.

From budgets, forecasts, staff positions, and each role staff hold within the company, workplace health and safety, flow charts from farm gate to landing, manufacturing, labelling, packaging, warehousing through to dispatch.

These were some of the policies I had to implement:

- Website privacy
- Ethical sourcing
- Social media
- Anti-discrimination and bullying
- Internet, email, and computer use
- Smoking
- English policy
- Hygiene and sanitation
- Employee confidentiality agreement.

I am sure many of the people working with us might have thought things were a bit chaotic, but the process of building a team to assist with this phase was essential. I had to focus on managing staff and putting people in charge of specific areas while Ken was busy building his own management protocols in production.

Ken and I had entered a precarious period in our relationship. We needed to compartmentalise our personal and professional lives to ensure we didn't become a casualty of our growing business success. It's easy to get caught up with the exciting developments around you and forget how and why it all began.

It was essential to remember the effort and sacrifice both Ken and I had made to get us to this stage. We had started as a dedicated and united team, and we'd lose it if we weren't vigilant.

Initially, our system worked well. However, with staff around us, new challenges arose. We had disagreements, especially when I was demanding Ken to slot in urgent orders. He had become structured in his product schedules.

Still, with the pressure I had always worked under growing the business and knowing how important some of these orders were to our cash flow, I had to press my case. I can hear some of you saying, 'What happened to structure?'

Without cash flow, there was no money to pay the weekly wages, regular containers of stock and packaging, and all the bills associated with the ever-increasing Factories of Dreams.

I had to be the driving force, juggling these different aspects of the business. I wasn't about to drop the ball and expect other people to drive our business; that responsibility fell on my shoulders.

I had delayed having our facilities registered for certified organic processing even though our farm in Fiji was certified organic. I had held off as long as possible, but the demand for organic products was growing, especially if we wanted to expand into overseas markets.

My decision was based on technicalities. We could sell and export bulk oil from the farm under their organic certificate and resell it as organic under their certification, as long as we didn't decant or repack the oil. Once we did, the oil lost its organic certification because our company and facilities were not registered as an organic processor.

The paperwork involved in upgrading to organic was extensive, including an organic handling plan, from the farm in Fiji through to manufacturing finished products in Australia. It gave me good practical experience in procedures that had to be implemented and put in place so that our production and overall business could progress.

The other areas of my focus in the company included staff management plans and more policies, including product recall procedures, instigating product liability and even more comprehensive insurance cover.

Ken was now working on production schedules to organise and plan our monthly stock levels. While his schedules were basic, they were vital in helping me manage overall purchasing and the supply of material we needed to meet demand. More importantly, to assist me in my ongoing juggling act with cash flow.

The building of our company structure had been essential to our growth. While we still might have seemed all over the place, and yes, even somewhat chaotic, behind the scenes I was very much in control and focused. Cashflow was number one on my priority list.

My wheels spun at a hundred miles an hour, and there was no way I was going to let them fall off.

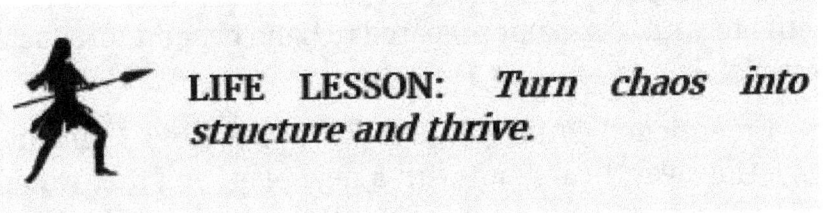

LIFE LESSON: *Turn chaos into structure and thrive.*

Finally, Mainstream Distribution

In the earlier days of our company's development, I'd decided not to go down the usual distribution sales channels. I wanted to do it my way!

I had known a good friend, Steward, for years. Our friendship went back to when Brynley was born. He had attended and video-recorded her christening. Over the years, Steward's company had become one of the state's largest health food distributors.

It was great to be able to give him a phone call and share ideas, even if he had a traditional approach to distribution. Distribution was what he was good at. Thank goodness we were good mates and respected each other enough to agree to disagree on my unconventional marketing approach.

With the sourcing of more raw material and increasing overheads, we had the capacity to supply more product. One of the points of contention with mainstream distributors was that, usually, they wanted exclusive rights over your brand or specific products for distribution statewide, or into certain territories.

With our products already selling so well online, and our growing customer base, regardless of my friendship with Steward, I was not prepared to hand over our products to a distributor.

I mentioned earlier some of the key reasons I felt this way. However, I came up with a new plan, one that would help provide us with a new sales channel, and at the same time not destroy or compete with our existing customer base. Part of the new plan was the addition of organic products to our range.

With the Fiji farm already certified organic, we implemented an organic handling plan and upgraded our facility's bottling, handling, and storage processes to upgrade to organic processor status. Even though we were using the same coconut oil, now with our new certification, we could pack and sell our oil with an organic logo.

This development also meant we had to pay organic levy fees and the additional expense of compliance and annual audits.

So how do you market the oil you've sold for years as non-organic and now substantiate a price increase to market it as organic?

My solution was in the packaging and creating a new sales channel. Finally, this is where Steward, my good distributor mate, came into the picture. I designed the new organic range in upmarket glass packaging, which would appeal to health-conscious consumers willing to pay more for organic products.

It was the ideal product line to launch through Steward's distribution network and not interfere with our existing, mostly online, consumer base. Steward was happy he now had the exclusive range he wanted.

After five years in business, we were selling through a new, conventional distribution channel. We had upgraded our Factories of Dreams into a certified organic processing facility. With Steward's sales channels, our new organic product range grew into a two million dollar a year brand for my friend and his distribution network.

We were so busy that Ken had implemented a night shift to keep up with demand and maintain stock levels. While we never hid the fact that our product came from the same source, one product carried certification with the necessary logo, while the other didn't and was more budget priced.

My initial concerns regarding confused branding proved baseless, and the new range, selling through retail outlets, was flying off the shelves.

I had Steward's experienced sales team to thank for the great job they did in marketing through these channels. I had no experience or expertise in these markets at all.

 **LIFE LESSON:** *Even when you do things your way, keep your mind open to all possibilities. You might be pleasantly surprised.*

We Made It – I think?

The definition of success can have so many different meanings. I believe our success was based on the fact that we were ahead of the game and had a direct link to and relationship with our supply source.

We had forged our own path, mainly because we were totally Cause-driven. Our focus was never on money. It was about creating products that reflected the traditional foods Ken's community had relied on for centuries.

The key was to identify these natural products and commercialise them to Australian food standards. At the same time, each label carried an important message, informing consumers about the plight of the Banabans, whom I classified as "the forgotten people of the Pacific". On average, we shipped around 100 online orders a day.

I didn't have time to worry about what others were doing. Who was trying to copy us? New competitors entering the market were resellers, and very few had the direct supply to source as we did. While others tried to incorporate a brand Cause, they were shallow, and it was more a marketing ploy than genuine.

At this stage, with so much additional growth, we had added Factory No. 4 to the Factories of Dreams within the

Since the injection of the additional $100,000 from Brian, our Dream Investor, the warehouse was bulging with stock. Unfortunately, with no racking, the bulk totes and steel drums were packed to the rafters.

It also meant our new forklift driver spent all day moving stock in and out and rotating stock at the same time. It was a labour-intensive process necessary to ensure stock was rolling over and not being forgotten or hidden.

It was amazing to see the additional stock flying off the shelves. In turn, the sales kept going up, which meant the cash was also rapidly increasing. Brian was over the moon every time he saw our financials.

While I thought I had to justify why we were bulging at the seams with more stock, he just smiled and said he had every confidence in what I was doing. As you can imagine, this type of investor is ideal, and I could not believe our luck. He genuinely believed in me and respected my judgement. He also never tried to assert his authority or opinion but instead became an excellent sounding board.

When your business is growing this fast, and your days in the office are like a whirlwind of activity, your brain, your thought processes, and your multi-tasking is also running at a million miles an hour.

I enjoyed all the challenges and the juggling of deadlines, finances, and staff. I fell into bed every night exhausted and slept the sleep of the dead.

Everyone around me never realised what was going through my head or the many different issues or levels of activity I was dealing with daily.

Over the years, I had been accused of jumping all over the place and not staying focused. In reality, it was how I was keeping up with the demands while my brain was on overdrive.

I also liked to spend some quiet time in the office after everyone left for the day, to catch up with work in a calm and peaceful space.

Regardless of how busy life had become, I still made a point of not working on weekends and not talking about business once I walked through the doors at home. I had to build my sanctuary around me to survive and, more importantly, to stop and reset my brain for the next day's challenges ahead.

Apparently, this is what success looks like.

Life on overdrive, the joy of everyday challenges, watching the sales tick over, and money rolling in, while more and more people rely on you to help support their families.

I loved it!

LIFE LESSON: *You can be so busy being successful that you never have time to enjoy it.*

Palace of Dreams

By 2013, we were nine years in, and the Four Factories of Dreams were overflowing. To grow to the next level and take on some of the new overseas distribution contracts I was developing, we would have to upgrade our processing facility to a higher food-grade level.

This step meant acquiring HACCP Certification (Hazard Analysis Critical Control Points), an internationally recognised food safety program. With all the procedures and protocols I had already implemented, we were already close to complying.

The timing was excellent, as the government had already offered us various manufacturing incentives. One of these was funding to help implement HACCP certification and the associated staff training required.

We had no problems qualifying for the grant, however during talks it became clear that the main food manufacturing section of our business would need to change.

Another episode resulted from the federal government incentive. Our company had gone through an audit to identify areas in our manufacturing that could benefit from government assistance.

During this process, the audit team was impressed with our Banaban Cause as the main reason behind our brand and the impact we were making financially and opportunity-wise for our farmers back in Fiji.

While we were waiting for approval from Canberra, I received a phone call from Jone. The staff at the Australian High Commission in Fiji requested a visit to his farm.

After hosting the group for the day, showing them his operations and discussions about supplying us in Australia, Jone wondered why the Australian government was interested in our business dealings.

I explained it was part of our audit process, and the team was impressed with the story behind our manufacturing. Obviously, they wanted to make sure we were genuine and not creating marketing spin. Jone laughed, stating, 'Well, whatever you told them, got them interested enough for them to fly all the way up from Suva.'

Our funding was approved the following week, and work on implementing HACCP began. But why was HACCP such a big step, and what did it really entail?

HACCP incorporates and identifies all types of food safety threats, from the floor, wall, ceiling coverings, light fittings to water and air quality, sanitising and equipment, staff clothing, and safe food handling. Even our warehouse, packing and storage areas had to comply. Our Four Factories of Dreams would need upgrades in all these areas. With four separate landlords and major renovations required, the Four Factories of Dreams would never cut it.

One afternoon on my way home, I noticed a fantastic showroom and warehouse for sale or lease about 3.2 km from our premises, on the main road. Ken happened to be away in Fiji at the time, but the moment I saw the building, I went online to check it out.

It was perfect for us. It was a corner block with two entrances, a large warehouse facility and a showroom area. Unfortunately, it was double the rent we were paying for our four factories. However, this building could showcase all things Fijian and Banaban.

The facility could be utilised for training, receptions, and even a cafe and test kitchen to highlight our coconut food and products. The whole upstairs area could become open offices, and it had a good-sized boardroom.

The building was a Palace of Dreams, where everything we were doing could be housed under one roof and designed perfectly to suit our needs.

We had just paid off Brian and asked him if he wanted to reinvest in our new set-up. He had already made $30,000 profit on his initial $100,000 investment and purchased storage facilities in New Zealand. He had his eye on a similar set-up here in Australia. Our turnover had more than doubled over the past eighteen months and was close to doubling again. We were cashed up, and my skills of juggling cashflow were finely honed.

Our stock had about a six-week turnaround from the time our bulk raw material arrived and was packaged. We had no wastage, as we now had developed products to ensure that every ounce of our raw material was used.

We had sales channels at different levels except for one –mainstream supermarket chains. With Steward's distribution channels, our products were now available in grocery stores. They were smaller family chains that had excellent regional distribution. He also supplied chemists and health food stores throughout Queensland and Northern New South Wales.

We had a Western Australian distributor who was doing very well. Adelaide distribution was just coming on board, while our Melbourne and Victorian distributors were relatively slow in comparison. Our Sydney distributors were somewhat troublesome.

16. With the Palace of Dreams. The four factories were now all in one facility.

The first one had gone into liquidation, and luckily for us, only owed us a few hundred dollars. We took on another New South Wales distributor, which we soon found was more focused on food sales.

Grocery distribution was a different ball game for us, and one which Steward was very good at. I wasn't a fan of the grocery market, as it was a competitive marketplace where sales pricing varied up and down like a roller coaster.

The profit margins were much lower than what I was used to. While this was a significant part of our distribution, I found it the lowest rung on our distribution ladder. It was the opposite of our more lucrative online and health food markets.

I spent the following weeks in serious discussions with the real estate agent and the owners of the premises up the road. Finally, I was able to negotiate a lease on the new Palace of Dreams. Our new premises and more importantly, the setup was not going to come cheaply.

While I realised we would be required to pay at least a month's rent in advance, our new landlord wanted a $75,000 security bond. The idea of having to put my hands on so much cash was daunting.

The bank would hold the money as security in a non-investment account. It could not be used as collateral or borrowed against. That amount was nearly equivalent to a full container of raw material that I could usually flip in about six weeks and virtually triple its value.

I negotiated the amount back to half that figure, but it still hurt to lose such a chunk of cash and assign it to the no man's land of the banking world for the entire time of residing in our new premises.

The next step was to undertake an extensive fit-out before we moved in. Over the coming months, the new Palace of Dreams took shape. Ken was in his element designing his new production rooms to HACCP food standards, and we ended up with a beautiful, purpose-built, state of the art facility.

Unfortunately, the downside was the blow to our cash flow, with a fit-out at a cost of around $250,000.

We finally moved the last of our four factories across to the Palace of Dreams in time to celebrate our company's tenth anniversary.

I organised a grand opening event, and some of our overseas and interstate distributors flew in. Other special guests included Fiji's High Commissioner, who flew in from Canberra, other federal government dignitaries, and the local Fijian community. We sponsored Banaban guests who we flew in from Fiji.

We rolled out the red carpet and put on a wonderful opening ceremony hosted by one of our supportive academic friends, Grant McCall. He had been a long-time supporter of our Banaban Cause. Our program highlighted Fijian and Banaban culture and dancing, and our local Fijian church choir performed the traditional Fijian farewell.

There were two other highlights for the evening. My ninety-year-old mother, who had always been such tremendous support to us over the years, performed the cake cutting ceremony. We had commissioned a large coconut shaped cake to commemorate our company's tenth year in business.

The other major part of the evening was the official launch of my youngest daughter, Brynley's book, *Going Coconuts*. Brynley had just turned twenty-three and had written and designed a fantastic cookbook, featuring our brand story and based on our products. Again, another one of our supportive academic friends, Max Quanchi, who had seen Brynley grow up over the years and had always encouraged her ambitions, hosted this segment of the evening.

Our dreams finally had come true, and the proof of our hard work was a reality. The Banabans now had a building and cultural centre representing them in Australia and on the world trading stage.

All our children worked with us except for two. Ken's eldest daughter, Ioanna, was back home in Fiji, looking after the family interests. My son, Aidan, pursued his career in the Australian Federal Police while offering his support in the background. One of Aidan's roles had been working throughout the Pacific region. He was keenly interested and supportive of the Banaban Cause.

Ken and I wanted the Palace of Dreams to represent the Banaban community and their plight for justice, and to highlight their traditional skills. We didn't want our facility to become another Taj Mahal and not benefit Ken's people back home in the Islands.

Ken was in his element with his custom-made machinery. He was busy running everything to our new HACCP food requirements while still maintaining our organic processing standards. We had a great team of around 28 staff now working with us, while our traditional Fijian *bure* (grass hut) set up on our ground floor hosted Brynley's marketing and design team.

The new era of Banaban virgin coconut oil had begun.

LIFE LESSON: *When your hard work starts to pay off, don't lose sight of your Cause or mission and why you started your business in the first place.*

The Price of Success

With so much expansion happening, we purchased a brand-new, state-of-the-art, shrink flow wrapper, which was custom made for us in Taiwan at the cost of around $100,000.

I designed a new one-litre plastic jar for our most popular product and contracted the manufacturer in China. Our one-litre plastic jars were being shipped by the thousands all over Australia, to some of the remotest locations.

The packaging had always been an issue for us, with the oil expanding and liquifying in the heat, then shrinking and setting solid when the temperature dropped below 18°C.

Now we had a robust, sealed and totally wrapped jar that could stand extreme conditions. It also made our branding stronger than ever before and unique, making it difficult for anyone to copy. I was now ordering 42,000 one-litre jars at a time, packed into a 40-foot container.

I also designed food pouches to match our new food products branding, and we were getting thousands of them manufactured in China. All these new packaging developments meant significant investments.

We had begun to host events at our new Palace of Dreams; cooking demonstrations, yoga classes, fitness classes, and we incorporated events with the local Banaban and Fijian communities.

We finalised our HACCP food certification with the necessary staff training, but we had to re-certify the new premises for Organic and Kosher certification, due to the move. This meant our recent audit and annual renewals were null and void, and we had to start the whole process again.

There were other hidden expenses we never expected. All our existing packaging no longer complied with Australian consumer laws.

We had thousands of dollars' worth of pre-printed food pouches, shrink-wrapped film, and hundreds of different product labels. They all had to be changed to the address of the new premises.

We began an expensive manual over-labelling process. Meanwhile, we recruited a graphic artist to join our staff to upgrade all our packaging.

Our packaging was worth well over $200,000 and it was not an easy or cheap fix.

Luckily, we had kept one of our old factories and our Italian friend was using it for his production for two of the products he provided for us. This gave us an additional six months to comply with a lawful presence at our old premises. It was also during this time that some other changes were happening behind the scenes.

Online sales were still strong, averaging around one hundred orders a day. We had more wholesale and distribution channels. Most of our wholesalers paid upfront, knowing we didn't carry accounts, while the distributors paid monthly.

Our main distributors were good payers. We knew their payments would be there at the end of each month. However, some of the smaller distributors proved unreliable and needed to be reminded, which was something we were not used to.

We had been blessed for the past ten years with fantastic cash flow, and we didn't need to have someone on staff to chase debts. We only ever had one bad debt for a couple of hundred dollars that had to be written off when the distributor had gone into liquidation.

With all the money spent on the move and new fit-out, I made a serious mistake paying for it all out of our cash flow. Con, my accountant, had taken on a new partner and merged his business with a big firm out of Sydney. Unfortunately, his wife contracted cancer, and the situation was grave.

Con had to reduce his working hours as his wife fought for her life during the following months. Meanwhile, his new partner flew up from Sydney for meetings. Due to our business's size and value, he immediately took it upon himself to take over our account's management.

While he was an experienced accountant, I found out later his specialty had been in the timeshare industry. He had no experience at all with manufacturing and product distribution. Con, who had been on the journey with us from the beginning, and more importantly, had believed in me, was pushed to the side.

Con thought he didn't have the accounting experience or expertise we needed since becoming such a large company. He told me years later that this was one of his greatest regrets. Still, to put it bluntly, I inherited an idiot who knew nothing about our business.

Our new accountant would write fancy 20-page reports on all the information I provided to him every quarter. He'd fly in from Sydney with one of his clerks in tow and sit in my office and tell me how well we were doing while going through the reports.

When I asked him for advice on the level of tax we were paying, he'd tell me that it was good as it showed we were making money. Really? Tell me something I don't know. What about advice on our cash flow, budgeting and purchasing flows? He just said he would look into it and get back to me.

What a waste of my time and money. Ninety minutes of my time that I would never get back. But I'd definitely be charged for every minute of it!

I immediately got in touch with Con and told him how unhappy I was. I was being hit with ridiculous accountancy bills in the thousands and not receiving any advice. Con wasn't happy with the merger either, or that he had been removed from our account. I gave him the list of questions I had presented to his colleague and sent him my end of year figures and the large tax bill I was facing.

Con could only talk to me as a friend now, and I pleaded with him to check out my figures. One glance and he asked why my packaging was sitting in "stock on hand" and not listed as a "cost of goods expense"?

This simple accounting error that the genius had overlooked may explain why I was still waiting for him to get back to me with the questions I had raised.

Apparently, when accountants don't know the answers, they pay about $400 to get advice from an accounting advisory body. They then pass the information back to the client after adding their fees on top.

While Con had to remain my ex-accountant due to his contractual agreements, we remained great friends. I still valued his opinion, even when it was limited. Meanwhile, the genius tried to get me to sign off on my end of year tax lodgement. I rang him and started to challenge him regarding his tax estimates and let him know I wouldn't sign off.

He advised he was flying up and would meet with me in person. I just kept thinking that I was footing his travel expenses to provide me with the wrong information.

When he arrived, I asked him about my packaging status in our books. I noticed that my question had hit a raw nerve. Even his clerk was squirming in his seat next to him.

I could see he was shocked that I had found the error and just saved our company over $30,000 on our tax bill. He worked overtime, trying to put a spin on what was his careless mistake. I told him to correct his figures before I'd sign the documents for lodgement with the tax office. I also asked him why he never advised me about financing the $250,000 for the fit-out for the new premises?

Again, this caught him off guard. He meekly replied that he never realised it was an issue or something I wanted to do. I replied that I thought it was strange that other business colleagues had offered that advice as the best option for tax purposes and to save valuable cash flow.

As he absorbed all I was saying, he meekly replied that I could still do that if I wanted to.

LIFE LESSON: *Ask your accountant what advice they can offer to help offset your tax and manage cash flow and expenditure. If they tell you, they will get back to you – warning bells! You need to find a new accountant.*

17. Brynley visiting Jone's organic coconut farm in Fiji with over 800,000 coconut trees before Cyclone Winston

CHAPTER 8

CAN WE HELP YOU SPEND YOUR HARD-EARNED MONEY?

As soon as the paperwork was lodged for our tax return, I advised him in writing that we no longer required his services.

He was so confident of my relationship with Con and so out of touch with me as a client that he could not believe I sacked him. He thought our business was working so well that he assumed it would be easy to just sit back and compile reports after the event and get well paid.

Well, the gravy train had just come to an abrupt stop. From that day on, my opinion of accountants waned. In fact, this episode was only the beginning of what was to come.

I spent the following months researching the finance for our $250,000 fit-out. Unfortunately, our builder was not happy to submit an amended invoice to cover the total amount.

It was now a year since the fit-out, and he had already submitted his tax return for the year. We had paid him staggered payments as each section of work was carried out.

There were other contractors involved, including electricians and air conditioning technicians. It was proving too difficult to bring all the paperwork together that I needed to secure finance.

I explored other options, but now with such an increase in sales, staff, and overall productivity, I needed to concentrate on boosting our cashflow to meet the growth.

LIFE LESSON: *The world is full of experts. But can they provide you with the right advice you need to justify the fees they charge for their professional services?*

What is Debtor Finance

To address the need for more funding, I had already increased our bank overdraft to fund more raw material we needed. Now I realised just how much the $250,000 fit-out and the security bond had dented our cash flow.

After making a few enquiries, I received a recommendation from the adviser I was working with under one of the government business initiatives. He put me in touch with Cash Resources, a company in Brisbane that offered debtor finance.

What exactly is debtor finance? It is a way to fund your business by using your accounts receivable ledger as collateral.

It was quite an involved procedure to set up, and required detailed information on our finances and sales turnover. After submitting all our paperwork, Cash Resources engaged an auditor to go through, double-check and confirm our company's financial position.

We had no problems with our turnover level, and once approved, our company was assigned a $250,000 trading limit.

This meant that instead of waiting thirty days or longer for account receivable payments to come through, we could draw down on our funds almost immediately. As soon as we produced an invoice and a signed delivery docket to confirm the goods were sent and received, the payment would be deposited into our account the next day.

Because we had consistent monthly accounts and some regular large bulk sales, this worked well for us and freed up funds immediately. Our debtor finance was only eligible for Australian sales and couldn't be used for international sales. The only drawback was if our customers defaulted on their payment, we were still liable. The longer customers took to pay or went over their 30-day trading terms, we would pay more interest.

For some companies, this could be a costly expense. Thankfully, I had always had stringent controls on the handful of account customers we had. I only allowed trading terms for a few of our bulk customers and distributors. If they started to fall outside our agreed terms, we preferred not to deal with them. The other important aspect of debtor finance is that your company still has the responsibility to chase your payments, not the finance company. For our company, working with Cash Resources became a great collaboration.

Every six months, we were audited to make sure everything was above board. Generally, we drew down around $160,000 on our accounts every month. Occasionally this could increase to around the $250,000 level. It was reassuring to know that this money could be freed up straight away. Cash Resources also allowed us great flexibility, unlike other debtor finance companies that were around at the time.

An added bonus – the company's Queensland sales manager, Roger, was supportive. Cash Resources was also a well-established family-owned business, and I believe this helped our two companies work well together.

Before making my final decision with Cash Resources, I had a meeting with one of the major banks that also offered this type of financing.

Their program was different, in that they insisted on taking over all our customer accounts and payments and running them through their debtor finance. There was no option to only factor the accounts I needed to. They wanted all our customers' money to go directly to them.

In other words, I would have to convert all our cash sales into accounts, which was ridiculous. Ninety per cent of our sales were cash sales. There was no way I was going to jeopardise those cash sales to get some additional bank funding. I politely thanked them and showed them the door.

This same bank was hit hard during the global financial crisis that followed, and many businesses had their debts called in overnight. I was relieved we weren't one of their customers.

Some of the other companies we worked with were not so lucky, and I know the stress this bank put them under as they had to source new funding. Not an easy feat in the middle of a global financial meltdown.

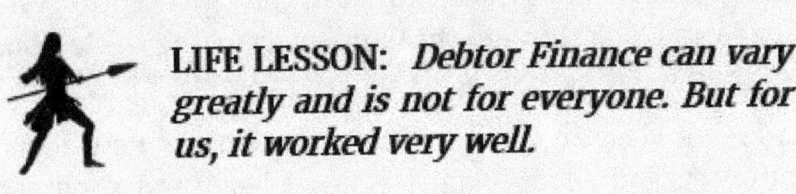

LIFE LESSON: *Debtor Finance can vary greatly and is not for everyone. But for us, it worked very well.*

Life Back Home in the Islands

Over the years, we supported various aid projects back on Ken's Island, especially the Children's Welfare program. Unlike Australia, primary and secondary education in Fiji wasn't free. Families had to pay $40 for school fees, plus the added cost of a school uniform, stationery, lunch box, and backpack. It all added up to a significant expense, especially in such an impoverished community.

A young Banaban woman started the program to assist other families in need. She had experienced the trauma of growing up with a father who couldn't provide for their family due to mental illness.

It broke my heart hearing about all the cases of hardship. Some parents had to decide which child they could afford to send to school and who would have to stay home and forgo an education.

Our company had to get behind this project, and over five years, the project had expanded to include the island's only high school. We sponsored the education of over 200 children on Rabi Island annually.

The story of one young eight-year-old boy was poignant. His parents could not afford to send him to school, yet he was so keen to learn that he used to stand outside and look through the window watching the lessons.

After we sponsored him, he proudly marched into the grade one class in his new uniform with his new school stationery and school bag. He stood head and shoulders above the rest of the class. He did not care that he was amongst all the five and six-year-olds, as his dream of attending school finally became a reality.

Meanwhile, Fiji's Department of Industry and Trade became aware of the coconut farm's export income generated with sales to us in Australia and the United States. Jone's farm was established in the 1870s, was multi-generationally owned and situated on the island just 14 miles away from Ken's Island of Rabi.

The farm had over 800,000 organic coconut trees planted, and had good access to essential local inter-island shipping; something our island of Rabi sadly lacked.

The government had been planning on building a wharf on Rabi over the past seventeen years. With us opening so much trade opportunity in this remote north-east region of Fiji through the newly-emerged virgin coconut oil industry, the government finally decided to complete the project.

Jone's large commercial farming operation employed more than 20 Banabans from Rabi and provided housing for their families.

During the growing season, the farm coordinated with different Banaban village youth groups. The young people came across to harvest coconuts, to earn money to fund their village projects. It was a win-win situation for many back home on the Island.

It also resulted in other communities benefiting from the demand for coconut oil and food products. In Vanuatu, many village farmers in the north were now supplying coconuts for oil production, while coconut food products were being made for us in Sri Lanka.

In Sri Lanka, we heard about a farmer who had upheld his traditional skills to harvest the coconut syrup, toddy. Just the same as Banabans had been doing for centuries.

The Banabans called their product *Ka maimai*, while the Sri Lanka farmer could only sell his product locally to manufacture their traditional alcohol called *arrack*. The other villagers thought he was crazy to uphold this old skill and were not interested in joining him.

Once we started buying all the syrup he could produce, the other villagers saw that his financial situation had changed and wanted to join him. It was so good to know these traditional skills were becoming valued and could make such a difference to the local economy.

The other significant development was the Fijian government finally realising the value of coconuts to their local impoverished communities, especially on their remote islands where coconuts grew abundantly, and the communities had no income.

The government undertook a Virgin Coconut Oil training program and used our Island of Rabi as their model. They assisted by building a small factory and provided initial

18. Stacey's son Aidan looking at some of the company's export markets and aid projects.

funding to get it started. We sponsored the project with some machinery, packaging, labels, and fragrances.

With plans underway for our new Palace of Dreams opening ceremony, we offered to bring two Banabans over for training at our facility. The local Rabi Island council nominated Terikano Takesau to manage the project on behalf of the women interest groups on the island.

Terikano soaked up knowledge while she was with us in Australia and learned all the different levels of marketing, margins, and budgeting.

Unfortunately, the Fijian government and their management team behind the establishment of the Fijian village projects told everyone that the oil was worth FJ$20. a litre. Obviously, they were guided by all the online marketing we were generating for our Banaban products in Australia and had no understanding that these were retail prices.

The management team didn't take wholesale, distribution and bulk pricing levels, and more importantly, export pricing into consideration. They had no idea that to export virgin coconut oil, it had to be made to a high food standard. It needed to pass all the regulatory food standards in different countries. The oil had to be packed in export standard bulk packaging, on export grade pallets.

They would need to produce 20,000 litres of high food-grade oil to fill a 20-foot container. If all these requirements were met, they had to find a way to arrange and manage inter-island cargo to get the products down to the main Suva port.

None of the above was viable, especially for such remote island manufacture. But what was feasible and sustainable was supplying local markets and the other smaller markets in Pacific countries, focusing on coconut body products.

To assist the women's project, with Jone's assistance we initially sponsored the import of various 200-litre bulk shipments when they were available. All Terikano had to do was get the oil they produced packed in 20-litre drums, and shipped across to Jone's farm. Jone donated the export totes they needed and packed the oil into the export shipping containers he sent to us.

The island's local boat hire to get over to Jone's farm added a high cost to the shipment. Even with our aid and sponsorship, the shipments were still three times the price of what was viable for the Australian market.

We continued to sell their oil under cost price as part of our support for the village. However, we realised for this important Island project to survive, it had to be sustainable.

They needed to find smaller markets locally that would work with their limited production. Regular customers and markets that would not stress them to produce high volumes that would never be viable for the Island project or us in Australia.

To Terikano's credit, she did just that.

The Banaban Virgin Coconut Oil project in Rabi has survived for seven years now and has become a model of what can be done to make a village project work, proving that it is not just sustainable but can thrive once aid funding dries up.

 **LIFE LESSON:** *The best markets for your products can be in your own backyard with smaller volumes and better profits.*

Success Now Our Enemy

From the moment we moved into the Palace of Dreams, a new chapter of our business began to unfold. With the increased production, storage and visibility that our new premises offered, more opportunities came our way.

With our new HACCP certification, more export opportunities opened up. But underlying all the excitement, a dark underside was beginning to fester.

We had reached our tenth anniversary in business, our products were everywhere, and all the years of marketing were finally paying off. But it was the first time that some negative incidents started to manifest out of left-field; totally unexpected. We already had started to see a lot more coconut oil brands starting up and trying to take advantage of all our hard work. Virgin coconut oil had now become a popular product.

Many of the new consumers had no knowledge of the years of blood, sweat and tears we had put into developing and marketing our brand. We even had some of the new "Johnny come latelys" trying to mimic our strong blue branding and beach theme.

There was confusion in the marketplace, mainly with new customers assuming the other blue labelled products were our brand. Luckily, we had trademarked our label image. Still, it only required some slight alteration to our design to get around that.

We had engaged a trademark attorney to assist us, and he was busy trying to protect our brand. As the saying goes, "imitation is the highest form of flattery" but it's also annoying when you have spent ten years creating and establishing a whole new coconut industry.

I had similar experiences when I had my flower shops. When you create something new and innovative, and people see your products everywhere, it soon puts a target on your back. The way I had always handled it in the past was to put my head down and focus harder on our work. I couldn't waste time and energy seeing what everyone else was doing.

You have no control over what other people do, but you certainly can be responsible for your own actions.

Another strange incident happened during this time when we had a visit from a government official from ACCC, the Australian Competition and Consumer Commission. Someone had made a complaint that we were falsely advertising that we were selling Fiji-produced oil.

The official was apologetic when he sat down in our boardroom and said we were obviously ruffling feathers with our success. He went on to say that the complaint was anonymous, and it was apparent someone was trying to make our business life difficult for us.

I told the ACCC official that our farm in Fiji had been inundated with supply enquiries out of Australia, and Jone had informed all of them that they only worked with us. I mentioned we had also brought on a new supply out of Vanuatu and Sri Lanka for bulk orders, and all this information was clearly defined.

He was blown away when I took him into my office and opened my export files. Every file was clearly marked and contained the paperwork and corresponding Certificates of Origin and Bills of Lading.

He saw how well organised we were, and he kept apologising, especially when I said, 'Please go and pick any one of our products off our shelves, and I will show you the corresponding paperwork.' He said he was so sorry to waste my time with what was obviously a vexatious complaint.

What was so interesting about this complaint was the fact our Fijian farm was the only organic, large, major-scale virgin coconut oil plantation and manufacturer in Fiji.

It was situated on an island in a remote region away from all the major towns and business centres. Except for the Fijian and Australian governments knowledge of the farm's export trade figures and the Fijian shipping agents knowing about the operations, we kept our business dealings between us.

No one had any idea of what the farm could produce and how it worked with our Banaban community back on Rabi. Of course, this leads to speculation and talk, especially when businesspeople in Fiji cannot access this market. They don't like to be blocked from becoming the middleman or controlling what is obviously a lucrative export market. People could only fixate on the success and not the years of trading that had been going on to get where we were.

Around this time, we were getting phone calls from Terikano, from the coconut oil project back on Rabi. She was telling us about traders starting to arrive on the island. Rabi is a closed community, not open to visitors or tourists without permission, so their visits were unexpected.

When these traders saw that the Women's project was a small island set up, and the Banaban brand name and labels (these were the thousands of old labels we had donated to the project), they assumed this was our company's main processing plant.

Jone's organic coconut farm was situated on the island across from Rabi and was a private family-owned business. He kept it closed to the general public while our Banaban workers and village youth groups travelled back and forward between the two islands.

Jone often would phone me to complain that more and more tourists were turning up at his front gate. The farm's location was in a remote area of the island, away from the main town areas. Jone and his team were flat out, trying to keep up with my orders and manage the hundreds of workers and their families living there.

He was becoming wary of people wanting to visit his farm to 'sticky beak', as he called it. He believed they were trying to find out how he was processing so much oil for large export shipments. My suspicion about people trying to break into our Fijian supply chain was confirmed a few months later.

Apart from potential competitors in Fiji, there was still an unknown person who had laid a complaint in Australia. Whoever that was would not have been happy when their complaint was deemed vexatious by ACCC.

Next, I received a phone call from a woman who was obviously an Indo-Fijian. She wouldn't give me her full name but claimed she was a friend of the Banabans in Fiji and was unhappy that I was exploiting them. Her words were like a red flag to a bull as I called on every ounce of my strength to hold my tongue and let her shoot her mouth off.

It soon became apparent that she had no idea who we were, our connections familywise and professionally in Fiji, and what we were doing. She started saying that she was a close friend of Terikano and the Banabans and helped them with their projects. Really?

I let her go on and on as she dropped more names. Luckily, she could not see me smiling on the other end of the phone. She had no idea that the people she had named happened to be our Island family members. I made a point of staying silent, and she finally asked me if I was still there? I politely asked her if she had finished and ever so calmly and nicely put her straight.

She was left speechless when I told her she must not really know the Banabans or our connections as we had been working with the community for nearly twenty years. She didn't even realise Ken was a Banaban and Terikano was his niece. I let her know that all the other people she had mentioned were Ken's relatives. This finally got her to shut up long enough to realise she had stepped into a hornet's nest. She had no idea we sponsored the Banaban project.

I hated the fact I had to justify ourselves to the likes of this woman. Her phone call seemed to suggest that she had made the complaint, as she mentioned she lived in Australia but had her business back in Fiji. She also confirmed that she had tried to visit Jone's farm. She wasn't happy when Jone had made it clear they were not interested in doing business with her. Instead, she was told to contact us in Australia.

After this episode, I realised how vulnerable our home Island Women's project was becoming. The phone call I'd just had was an ominous sign that there were forces determined to undermine our business in Australia. I spoke to Terikano to explain what was going on. Because of the nature of their project and the Fijian government's support, it meant all their information was publicly available.

Terikano was just so grateful for any assistance they received and believed she had to show transparency and run the operation as an open book.

Terikano was so excited at the idea of more sales.

There had even been different business traders turning up from Suva, wanting to buy bulk from them and making big promises. She was just so innocent and trusting and unaware that people were good at promising you the world.

In business, talk was cheap. It was all part of an ongoing learning curve and introduction to the tough and ruthless business world. I was more worried about these traders buying oil produced by the women and label it as genuine organic, Banaban oil. The Rabi Island oil was sun-dried and a handmade product, very different to what we were selling in Australia.

Of course, these vultures and opportunists had no idea of that. They just wanted to trade off our name.

The Island project could only produce a small quantity of oil. Still, it didn't stop unscrupulous traders blending it with other rubbish out of Fiji to try and crack our Australian markets. I decided the only way to protect our business was to offer to take all the bulk oil our small island project could produce at an inflated price, to keep all our oil inhouse.

After exporting to us for eighteen months, all the additional costs were adding up. Not only did Terikano have more added upfront production costs, but the team also had to produce bulk oil at much lower margins. It required a massive number of coconuts to fill these larger orders.

Finally, the team on the Island understood what I was saying. It was not about getting larger bulk orders that would never be viable or sustainable for them but building a more lucrative local market with better margins; orders and sales they could manage and grow to match their limited capabilities. This is the main reason few aid projects work on a long-term basis. Once the aid and assistance dries up, the projects usually fall over and are not sustainable.

While it was hard weaning our continued funding from the project, I made it a slow, gradual process. First to go was the imported fragrances, which were replaced with innovative new Island-made natural fragrances.

Next, they worked on designing their own labels and printing them in Fiji. I gave them copies of all our packaging artwork to assist them in the changeover. Terikano's dedication to the project never waned, and she put in a lot of time and effort to develop new local markets.

Her tireless networking efforts with the local Fijian government and Pacific agencies paid off. She has been the driving force behind the project.

Another strange episode happened during this period when people walked into our downstairs showroom and asked if the business owner was in. It just so happened I was downstairs in reception at the time and went over and introduced myself as the owner. They seemed taken aback and said they had met the gentlemen who owned the business and asked if I was one of the partners?

Ken also happened to be walking past and came over to join us. I introduced him as my partner and husband, and they were even more taken aback. They said, 'Oh, we must have met your other owner, the one that lives on Tamborine Mountain selling spring water.' Ken and I looked at each other puzzled. I explained Ken and I were the sole owners of our business, and we had no partners, no investors, no shareholders etc.

They were embarrassed and apologetic and explained the misunderstanding. The man they had met had been telling potential investors in his spring water business that he was a major shareholder of our company. And he had put it, 'You will see our big premises on the main road at Burleigh Heads.' Obviously, he hadn't expected people to turn up at our premises to check us out.

The couple's "homework" had paid off. They came through the door so excited, earnestly believing they would be getting involved with an investment group, with our business as part of the portfolio.

After we gave this lovely couple a reality check, they left our premises very despondent. Still, I hope they realised just how lucky they were to discover the truth in time before investing with someone trading on lies and fabrication.

This episode highlighted that, when it came to business, people were capable of anything. I had already experienced so many unbelievable incidents over the years. Still, the Palace of Dreams seemed to be like a magnet, drawing different types of wheelers and dealers through our front door. Unfortunately, our success and our great new premises had put a spotlight on everything we were doing.

The target on our backs seemed to be growing bigger by the day.

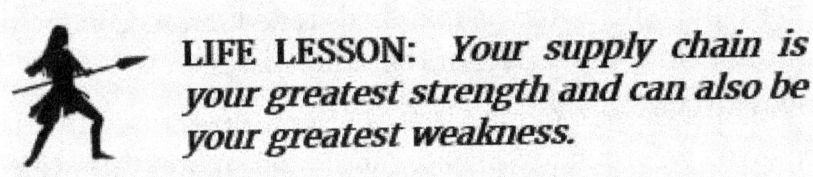

LIFE LESSON: *Your supply chain is your greatest strength and can also be your greatest weakness.*

Success – a Two-Edged Sword

With the Palace of Dreams functioning so well, we also utilised the facility for various community activities and trade events. I worked closely with the export division of our local council. We offered our facility to host multiple overseas trade missions, creating some great new opportunities.

Another exciting development was our involvement with the Food for Medicine programme and the research team from the University of Southern Queensland, Toowoomba.

Our company had sponsored one of their research food scientists to work with us as part of a two-year Federal government initiative – Researcher in Business. The objective was to scientifically prove the health benefits of coconut oil and some of the other new coconut products we had developed.

When we started the business, Ken often mentioned how they used coconut traditionally back home on the Island to treat different ailments. I had to remind him that we could never make such health claims for fear of being shut down here in Australia. It took quite a while for Ken to get his head around how strict Australia was in this regard, especially when his people had relied on coconut for centuries in every aspect of their daily lives.

While we put money into research, working with the experts, we found we had more and more "so-called experts" wanting to help us. Many of them had no idea we had been at it for over ten years, or that our business had been created online at a time when eCommerce was in its infancy. They didn't know that I had ignored traditional marketing models until we were ten years down the track. I had built our own markets and our way of doing business.

For our unconventional grand opening, we engaged a public relations company and subsequently, they were put on a $4,000 monthly retainer on a twelve-month contract. It worked out that the cost of the agreement was worth the wage of an additional staff member. While it started well, I found that the PR company was only releasing one press release a month and had assigned a young undergraduate to handle our account.

In the end, I wrote most of the content, and the principal of the PR company supposedly edited and approved it. While they were professional and well-connected, the contract didn't live up to expectations. It also made me appreciate the value of the free publicity that had initially been generated with our brand appearing on various television stories.

While we were putting money into research and development and paying our PR firm to get our story and research out there, it became apparent that our efforts had become a two-edged sword.

My good intentions of educating the public about coconut's health benefits also benefited our competitors, who didn't spend one cent on building a market or putting money into research. We were opening the doors, more like the floodgates, as more smaller operators flooded the market. All they could see was our success story and our new fancy Palace of Dreams, and they wanted to jump on our coconut bandwagon.

Three years previously, I had discussions with a Woolworth's buyer about introducing virgin coconut oil into their supply chain. At the time, they believed virgin coconut oil was still an emerging market, but they were interested in receiving all the necessary supplier paperwork. It was at that time I realised there was no way I wanted to go down this route.

The more I researched the retail sales channel, the more I realised we'd end up competing against ourselves and the market we had already built. The other problem would be turning our excellent market into a cheap supermarket brand. More importantly, it would put a huge demand on our supply and resources. We would have to bring on new farmers and new countries just to supply the supermarket chains.

There was no way I could put that load on our Fijian farm. This was a critical decision I made then, and upheld. It was also a vital choice I made for the future of our brand and company.

There was another development around this time with our main natural health store chain we had been supplying for six years. They had a new CEO, and he wanted to develop their own in-store brands.

He quickly realised the number of sales and the amount they were spending on our products – especially our top-selling Fijian grown, one-litre non-organic virgin coconut oil.

The CEO phoned me and asked me to quote on contract packing our Fijian oil under their store brand. During our conversation, my mind was working overtime. I got off the phone, realising his request was huge and one I had to think very seriously about.

The one-litre product line alone with this group was worth around $25,000 a month without any of our other products in their monthly spend. There was a lot at risk, plus our ongoing working relationship with this chain.

While I understood the new CEO's reason for developing in-store brands of their most popular products, we could lose a major sales channel. We had to tread carefully. It could also allow one of our competitors to walk in and pick up all our hard-earned sales. I phoned the CEO back and asked if he was happy for us to quote on our virgin oil from one of our other island sources, not Fiji. He advised that their customers definitely wanted the Fijian grown oil.

Wow! That made my decision even harder. Meanwhile, a few days later, I received another one of those strange calls. This time from a food manufacturer in Sydney, I had met at one of the various food trade shows I had attended.

He informed me that not only did he supply his products to the same health food chain, but he also did some contract manufacturing for them. He went on to tell me that he had been asked to quote on supplying and contract packing Fijian produced virgin coconut oil. This phone call was odd.

I informed him that I had already been asked to give them a quote as we had been supplying them with our Fijian-grown oil for years. I wasn't sure if he'd been asked to phone me by the health store's CEO, or he was just on a "fishing expedition" to check out our position on this. At least I knew now they'd be using him to contract-pack their oil.

He kept prodding me to get a reaction out of me. He stated that the health food chain would source it from somewhere else, and I said they were very welcome to do that. Apparently, this was not the reaction he expected from me.

It took all my inner strength to stay calm and sound nonchalant. Not an easy feat, as he seemed to know a lot about our supply with this group. I added we were not concerned as our customers were loyal to the Banaban brand and had bought it through the company's health food stores for years.

He replied with a smart-arse comment that really hit a nerve and kept playing in my mind. He stated, 'Of course, if you supply them your Fijian oil for their in-store brand, they will tell their sales staff to tell the customers it is Banaban oil-packed under their brand and is cheaper!'

I politely ended our call and hoped I had not shown my hand, and more importantly, my concerns. Of course, he was right. If we supplied them our Fijian oil in bulk, they would do precisely that! So once again, it made my decision even harder. I procrastinated and pondered it more until finally, their purchasing officer phoned me to ask if I had their quotation ready. I knew I could not hold off any longer, and I finally put together my quote.

Yes, I would supply them our Fijian oil and contract pack it under their label, but my quote was for the exact same price we were charging them for our Banaban branded product.

I emailed the quotation off, and it didn't take long before I had the purchasing officer back on the phone. He thought I had made a mistake as I quoted the same price, they were already paying for our Banaban brand. I replied there was no mistake.

If they wanted us to supply our much sought-after Fijian produced oil, that was the price. I added that our company was not prepared to start a price war or compete against itself. If the company wanted a cheaper quote, we were happy to supply our Vanuatuan grown oil that was similar.

I had offered a compromise, hopefully not lost face, but at the same time standing firm on protecting our brand. It didn't take long before I had Jone from the farm phoning me complaining. He asked me what was going on? He had been receiving phone calls and numerous emails, asking them to supply oil to Australia. Of course, they received the same reply as always, to contact us directly in Australia.

With our tight business and Island relationship, other Australian traders and manufacturers soon discovered it was a closed shop. The local Fijian coconut oil market revolved around low-grade copra oil. The middlemen had no understanding of how virgin coconut oil was produced and how it had to be processed fresh within twenty-four hours from the time of harvest.

On Jone's farm, they had the coconut in the driers within hours. They harvested daily, starting at 5am and working to a midday deadline to ensure the oil's freshness. It was one of the essential aspects of the virgin coconut industry. The high-producing coconut farms are situated in remote, unspoilt regions away from the towns and cities, so having a specialised processing plant on your farm or nearby requires a lot of infrastructure.

In the traditional copra industry, coconuts need to be smoked or sun-dried to stop the coconuts from rotting. This process can result in the copra, as it then becomes known, turning a sooty, blackened colour. Remote indigenous coconut farmers take so much care in cutting and drying their coconuts.

It can take them months before they have enough copra ready to make the long and arduous journey to the nearest copra mill. Sometimes this can be hundreds of kilometres away.

Ken had been one of those farmers when he lived back home in his village. He knew the industry like the back of his hand. Ken lamented that after all his efforts to produce a clean, dry product, they would drop their copra on the mill's grounds only to see it sit out in all the tropical downpours that frequented the Islands. He wondered why he bothered when he watched dirty bucket of the front end loaders scoop up his copra to move it into the plant for processing.

When they finally squeezed the oil out of the copra, it produced a dark smoky-smelling oil. No wonder it had to be cleaned, bleached, or polished to make the oil safe to eat by removing the smoky smell and flavour.

Of course, for the buyers back in Australia, they had no understanding of this, just like the people who had turned up on our Island to check out the village project. So, even for Fijian middlemen and buyers to get their hands on commercially farmed and processed virgin coconut oil, it was a closed shop.

So, you ask what happened with the crucial decision I made not to compete with ourselves? The health food company did not take up my offer and put out its own brand in direct competition. I had another conversation with my Sydney contract packer friend. I heard they had finally had to use Sri Lankan produced oil. I told him I was happy to hear this. Again, he was taken aback by my positive response. I explained Sri Lankan oil was nothing like ours and would offer a different product for the customers.

Over the next three months, our one-litre bottle sales were significantly reduced as the health food chain flooded their stores with their new in-store range. They also threw a lot of advertising and marketing into their launch. Luckily, they were still ordering our other products and sizes as usual.

It took about six months before our one-litre bottle orders started to creep back up. We had noticed the health food chain was selling some other smaller brands as well, and the competition was increasing every day.

While the six months had hurt us, my decision to not compete against ourselves had paid off. Our sales returned to their regular monthly levels. They never increased past that point, but the main thing was our sales stayed consistent.

A year later, the purchasing office contacted me again to ask me if we would like to submit a quote to contract-pack our Fijian oil for their one-litre bottles. I happily told them we could, and once again, I produced the same quote I had given them the year before. We didn't get the job, and our sales didn't drop at all this time.

Many of you reading this will have pondered the stress and time required to make the hard calls, the hours spent working through how to negate the risks, and some of you will even work on the percentage of risk involved. I know there are smart people out there who will insist they can take the risk out of decision making. Well, that is all well and good, but all business, in the end, is high risk. We stand to make a lot of money if it works and lose a lot of money if it doesn't.

We can always take the middle ground, avoid all risk and drift along happy with the status quo. But my attitude is that to make a difference in whatever it is in business or life, you have to stand up and be counted.

Complacency has never been part of my thinking. Maybe I'm addicted to risk-taking and living on the edge. Still, I have developed a simple thought process that I finally close off on in my head after making a tough decision.

The percentages will always come back down in the end to just fifty-fifty. You will either make it or fail. It's as simple as that! Just make sure you also put some thought into your Plan B as a fallback position.

LIFE LESSON: *Think very hard about the tough decisions you need to make. Be prepared to stand by them and fall on your sword if things go wrong.*

Who Do You Trust?

Among all the joys and opportunities of working out of the Palace of Dreams, other events would significantly affect our business moving forward. It was the first real inkling that the wheels on our success bus had started to develop a wobble.

Up until now, everything we did or touched seemed to turn to gold. Except for my problems in finding an accountant whose abilities could match their fees, we had a great team of people around us, including our suppliers and staff.

We were like one large extended family, and we valued all our suppliers here in Australia and our overseas farmers.

It was a win-win situation for all of us working together. We were tight, and supported each other's back. Of course, there were the usual staffing issues, but these were minor when you considered our team's size and different cultural backgrounds. We overcame so much and raised our business to a much higher level of management and production that I was proud of.

Except for the new challenges that I've mentioned, I had another issue that came out of left field. It proved challenging, and needed all my strength and brainpower to navigate. This time it was generated over social media and felt "hate-driven" and something I had never experienced before. There had been publicity about Australian companies being halal registered, and it had turned into a campaign, saying Australian companies were sponsoring and supporting terrorism. Wow! How the hell was I going to manage this one?

Years back, when we first started, I had an export enquiry for bulk oil from our Fijian farm for Malaysia. They required the oil to be certified halal, and I spoke to Andrew, our old patriarch on the farm, to discuss the issue. He was already in his mid-eighties, and he didn't see it as being a problem. He had employed Indo-Fijians with Muslim origins back in the seventies.

The farm was self-sufficient, and with Fiji being predominately a Christian country, he had built a small mosque to accommodate some of his workers. Apparently, the mosque on the farm is the only one ever constructed and privately owned in Fiji.

At the same time, he built a Christian based school alongside the mosque for the workers' children. Andrew set up a meeting with the Island's local Imam to organise a certificate we would need for Malaysia. He was shocked when the Imam asked him for $6,000 for the certification. Andrew reminded the Iman that he had built and paid for their mosque at no expense to the local community. Seeing the mosque was situated on his land, he added that he would have to start charging the community for the use of the building.

Andrew's statement quickly resulted in the halal certificate being issued at no cost. Ironically, the Malaysian deal never came off, and we had long forgotten about it until this ugly episode raised its head. One of our earlier marketing documents outlying the background information on the farm and the fact it was the only certified organic coconut farm in all of Fiji with kosher and halal certification.

Now we had people on social media wanting to blacklist our company for supporting terrorism. To put it mildly, I felt sick to the stomach. Here I was trying to be open in my appreciation of different cultures, with the Island communities we worked with mostly upholding strong Christian values. At the same time, the farmers we worked with in Sri Lanka were mainly Buddhist. Who would have ever thought our company would get tossed in the deep end with such a hate group?

As I scrolled through a growing tirade of nasty posts, I couldn't help but wonder why we were targeted, especially when we had never registered our products as halal. After all the years of using social media for our benefit, we were now on the receiving end of cyberbullying. From my years of experience on social media, I had to take this seriously. I had to address the issue without getting roped into a tit for tat online argument or debate in any way.

My first response was to write a considered, restrained, and logical request to the various sites' administrators to remove the posts calling on members to boycott our company.

Secondly, I informed them that the information stated on their sites was incorrect and that none of the products we sold were halal certified. Thankfully, the administrators of the sites responded and removed the posts.

They even added a retraction after explaining that we were very much a multicultural Australian owned family business. I stated that our company supported all religious denominations. I added that our products only carried organic and kosher certification. I informed them we were currently working with the farmers from the Island's Fiji Catholic mission to upgrade them to organic growers to bring them into our supply chain.

This fact was at odds with what some of the posts were claiming about us supporting terrorism. I added that the posts on their sites had been misleading and damaging to our company's mission to support village communities throughout the Pacific.

I hated having to justify ourselves and bring religion into any areas of our business. We had customers of all denominations. However, I could not help but wonder how our company had been brought into this ugly smear campaign. Who had triggered such an attack on us?

Once again, I had this growing feeling there was more going on behind the scenes. It definitely felt like we were being targeted.

LIFE LESSON: *When handling problems created on social media, address them immediately. Stay calm and focused on the message you need to convey. Do not get involved in tit for tat online arguments.*

When Export Deals Go Wrong

While I encountered these various issues in Australia, I negotiated a major export supply contract for bulk organic coconut oil for a Canadian food manufacturer. The deal had come via Grahame, a New Zealand oil broker who had been in the food industry for years.

He had a good standing and reputation in the industry, and I had worked with him before. With Grahame involved, I knew it was a solid deal, and I put in a lot of effort to get it off the ground. Due to the potential size of the contract I had arranged, the oil shipments would come directly from our supplier in Vanuatu. This freed up our Fijian oil exclusively for our Banaban brand in Australia and gave our Vanuatuan growers export opportunities.

Vanuatu had much better capabilities to fill this large-scale ongoing supply contract. The Canadian manufacturer contract-packed for a major US supply chain and our coconut oil had to comply with Canadian and USA food standards. With such a substantial supply contract on offer, I had to meet up with Grahame and his Canadian client in Vanuatu. They wanted to inspect the manufacturing plant and be assured that Paul, who owned the operations up there, could fulfil the orders.

Our meeting went well, and I suggested starting with a trial shipment of just one, 20-foot container first. This first-order would allow them to ramp up supply and increase production as necessary over the coming months.

When we met our Canadian buyer in Vanuatu, he already had wanted to increase the first order to two, 20-foot containers. Now it meant the first order had just doubled to 40,000 litres of oil. Paul was beside himself, but I calmed him down and gave him a reality check. Before Paul could start, I had to arrange a full container load of empty 1,000-litre totes he needed for the export packaging. I organised for them to ship from Taiwan directly to Paul in Vanuatu.

Each Canadian shipment was worth around US$220,000, and Paul would have to outlay a significant amount of cash to his farmers to fill the orders. I had to remind Paul if something went wrong, there was a lot of money at risk.

With this in mind, I offered to fund the packaging shipment, and he could pay me back as he received money for each shipment.

Export packaging was always an issue for our suppliers in the Pacific and could really add to their production costs. By investing in full containers direct from manufacturers in Taiwan, it would reduce this cost by more than half.

Up until I started working with Paul, he'd struggled to find a market for his oil. The plant had hardly been operating, and he had to lay staff off and borrow money from the bank to stay afloat.

19. Stacey with the large carved drum made for her birthday feast in Vanuatu.

I could understand why he was excited at the prospect of a lucrative supply contract. I just had to make sure he didn't get ahead of himself and make sure he concentrated on the order at hand.

Our Canadian buyer was not helping the situation with his talk of now wanting to place a standing order for three, 20-foot containers every month.

While Vanuatu had massive coconut resources and farmers willing to supply, Paul's plant would have to run non-stop twenty-four hours a day to process this amount of volume.

Unlike Jone's well-managed and maintained operations in Fiji, Paul was a bit of a loose cannon with his management style. He was an expat who had spent years living in the tropics. He was married to one of the locals and had the added responsibility of supporting a young family.

Paul worked closely with various villages that had been certified organic. He'd built a great plant, and unlike Jone's Fijian plant that ran on steam generation, Paul's factory ran on coconut biofuel. Paul had a lifetime of experience and adventures and, along the way, had developed a drinking problem.

I got on very well with Paul and focused his mind and efforts back on business. At the same time, Ken developed a great working relationship with Paul's right-hand man and all the local village farmers, who appreciated our efforts to get the plant fully operational again.

The past eighteen months working with them had made a difference for the local community.

They had already shown us their appreciation when I celebrated my birthday while Ken and I were up there on one of our numerous visits. The whole village had turned up at the plant for a typical Island-style celebration of traditional dancing and accompanying feast.

The local Vanuatuan culture was fantastic, and the villagers had carved large Island drums especially for the occasion, that I then had the privilege of playing during the ceremony.

I realised the impact our work had on the locals when they all stood in line at the end of the night to thank me personally. From the oldest men and women in the village right through to the youngest, they stepped forward one by one to shake my hand and kiss me on both cheeks. I had forgotten about the French influence in Vanuatu, but obviously, the locals had embraced this French custom with enthusiasm.

As Paul's right-hand man explained, since we started working with them, they could send their children to school and support their families.

Ken enjoyed his time in Vanuatu, meeting with elders in the various villages. They related to him being a fellow Islander who had lived a traditional life, just like them, as a copra cutter. Ken loved being away from the big city smoke and fancy boardrooms.

While Vanuatu had an excellent supply of coconuts, processing such massive volumes would take a non-stop, twenty-four hour, seven days a week production schedule.

It would put increased strain on equipment. On average, a 20-foot container would require the harvesting and processing of at least 800,000 coconuts.

Just as Canada's first order began, unbeknownst to me, Paul was having problems with plant machinery. His lack of maintenance was now resulting in continued breakdowns.

The stress of finishing the order on time and staying on schedule was difficult. I sent Ken back to give them a hand and ensure they had the shipment ready to leave.

Ken flew home when they finished filling the forty totes, confident everything was on schedule. All they had to do was pack the two containers up at the plant and get them down to the wharf to meet the ship, arriving in the next few days.

It was a major mistake on our part. Ken should have stayed until the goods were packed into the containers and loaded onto the ship. While everything seemed to be straightforward, dealing in the tropical islands can change things quickly.

Days of heavy rain set in, and the dirt road to the plant had turned into a muddy track. One of the shipping containers made its way down to the wharf on the Island's only lift truck. It had just made it, nearly becoming bogged on its way. As the torrential rain continued, the shipping company insisted the remaining 20 totes for the second container would need to be packed on-site at the wharf.

Time was running out, and the ship was due the next day. Paul hired an open bed truck to transport the totes down to the port to avoid missing the ship.

It also meant that they had to load the totes in these extreme conditions, which unfortunately allowed water and mud to get on the pallets and moisture under the plastic outer tote wraps.

While I was back in my office feeling such a sense of relief, knowing that we had our shipment safely onboard, I wasn't aware of the last-minute panic.

I was busy focusing on getting our payment via a Transferable Letter of Credit (TLC) activated. It was my first experience dealing with a TLC, and I hoped my last. What is the difference between a Letter of Credit (LC) compared to TLC, you ask? I was soon to discover - a nightmare!

I was the middleman, and my Canadian buyer was under Grahame, his New Zealand agent. To further complicate the deal, I was acting as the agent for my Vanuatuan manufacturer. So out of the price I had negotiated with Grahame, he had his agency fee to come out of the payment, and I had my commission as well.

When negotiating trade deals at this level, you deal directly with the agent and vice versa. This is where a TLC payment is the best option. The Canadian buyer's bank transferred payment through to Grahame's New Zealand bank. Then his bank deducted his commission, and the balance was transferred to my bank in Australia.

When the money was finally cleared and released, I then had to pay my Vanuatuan supplier. Technically a Transferable Letter of Credit is supposed to save you time and resources in the process.

Wrong!

It took well over a month to go through clearance with each bank, and each word of the document was critically assessed for the tiniest mistake.

One of the main problems was that the original Bill of Lading had been sent to me via a well-known International Express courier service. Somehow it had disappeared in transit. No one could tell me where it had gone.

A regular two-day dispatch had turned into two weeks, and my patience had well and truly worn out. The Canadian bank wouldn't even start the payment process until they had the original Bill of Lading.

Finally, it eventually turned up, and the long process of transferring the funds through each country began. The last of the transfers finally cleared about two weeks before the goods arrived at the destination port in Vancouver. I was soon to discover another problem with the shipment when it landed.

My nerves were already frayed from the stress of getting this deal done and the payment released. I believed the pressure was finally off, and I was confident the quality of Paul's oil would meet the buyer's product specifications.

But that was not the problem. When they opened the second container, the cardboard totes had softened with moisture in the shipping container, and the metal pallet straps were rusting.

Paul had arranged for the Island's timber yard to make his export pallets with specially treated green copper oxide pine. While they were not export stamped ISPM15, he believed the certificate from the timber company would suffice.

The most significant problem using these types of pallets was that pine is softwood, not hardwood. It absorbed the moisture from being packed in wet weather and had turned mouldy.

With such a long sea voyage crossing the Pacific, the container's high humidity and moisture levels increased and weakened the outer cardboard tote casing. Combined with rough seas, it had resulted in the bottom layer of totes collapsing.

Thankfully, the oil contents remained intact in the bladders inside, but our Canadian buyer was not happy. First, he had to appease Canada's Food Inspection Agency (CFIA) as the container was quarantined on entry.

Next, he had the other pressing problem on how to transship the last 20,000 litres of oil over 1,200 km across the country with all the outer totes destroyed. It proved a costly exercise to rectify, and he had to pay for the goods to be repacked in Vancouver before the final leg of the journey.

Luckily for us, our customer was an experienced importer and utilised all his connections and resources, including his trade insurance, to assist him. Initially, due to the damage inside the container, they believed the seawater had breached the seals during transit. However, packing the shipping container in heavy rain outdoors would have also contributed to the issue over such a long sea voyage.

While I was busy trying to smooth over all the problems with our upset customer, Paul was back in Vanuatu, enjoying the fruits of his labour and exhibiting some very erratic behaviour. He decided his boiler at the plant needed replacing, so he purchased a second-hand boiler out of New Zealand, sight unseen.

Even before the new boiler had landed, he ripped out the old one and shut down the plant. This proved a huge mistake. When the new one finally arrived, he had to do a complete upgrade to the plant's electrical power board.

After a costly installation setup, the boiler wouldn't work.

After months of finally sorting out the Canadian export debacle, the Canadians were still interested in getting continued supply. But for me, the boiler debacle became the last straw.

I had spent thousands of dollars flying our own electrician from Australia to try and get it running and flew Ken up there to try and assist.

Even Jone from Fiji travelled over with me to see if he could help with his years of experience. He could not believe the number of coconuts lying on the ground all over the island and going to waste.

When he saw Paul's plant that had been initially set up at the cost of USD 2.4 million, he was in awe. But unlike Jone's operations, which were nothing like this scale, Jone's plant was much more efficient and ran continuously, day and night. It only stopped for scheduled monthly maintenance. He had permanent staff living on the farm in charge of all different aspects of his production. It was a well-managed operation.

After we invested more money trying to get Paul back on his feet, we realised he was also having other personal issues.

I had to cancel any future export sales. The level of stress and losing confidence in Paul was not worth my professional reputation in the industry. There was too much money at stake, and I always upheld the principle of only working with people that I totally trusted and had confidence in.

From that point on, I only worked on smaller shipments with Paul for our bulk supply back in Australia. The sad part about the whole affair was that due to the boiler issues, his supply to our Australian operations was now suffering. It took another twelve months for Paul to rectify his boiler stuff-up.

Meanwhile, all I could think of was the hundreds of local villagers around the island who had lost an excellent export deal, with all their coconuts going to waste, rotting on the ground. What a difference it would have made to the entire Island economy.

While in my heart I knew Paul's intentions were honourable and he cared for the people around him, sadly, the booze had won out.

LIFE LESSON: *When things are out of your control, try not to fixate on the loss but focus on the steps you need to recover.*

When Suppliers Let You Down

Our success put more strain on our supply chain.

Unfortunately, while the Canadian-New Zealand supply contract had collapsed in a heap, we were still waiting on Paul in Vanuatu to get back into production. I needed their oil which was similar to our Fijian oil, and I loved working with the local village growers up there.

Finally, we received word from Paul that they had 10,000 litres of oil to send us. Even though we had poured money into the packaging and assisting them, it would have to wait. Paul still needed us to help out by paying the total amount for the oil shipment to help them slowly get back to full production.

I sent the payment as usual and arranged with our shipping company to expect the shipment. While I had lost trust in Paul's ability to produce large export shipments, I never had an issue with him money-wise. Our business dealings had always been as solid as a written contract. Sadly, the situation changed.

I received a phone call from our shipping agent that Paul's shipment was not on the ship. It was not possible; I had a draft Bill of Lading. It had to be aboard!

Getting in touch with Paul was difficult, so Ken got on the phone, using his Island connections to see what the hell was going on. While they had taken nearly twelve months to get their boiler and plant restarted, Paul had accepted payment from a local buyer who had an export order for New Zealand.

Unlike us, the local buyer was not aware of the full extent of Paul's production problems at the plant. He had gone ahead and paid upfront for his NZ client's order months prior and was extremely upset. He, in turn, had an irate New Zealand buyer breathing down his neck and no oil.

20. Ken at the coconut farm in Fiji assisting with aid after Tropical Cyclone Winston's devasting impact.

When the buyer had heard via the Island's coconut wireless that ten pallets were down at the wharf awaiting shipment to Australia, he got the local police to intervene. They seized our oil on his behalf.

We were now out of pocket for 10,000 litres of oil that we really needed to back up our bulk supply. I could not fixate on the loss as it was something out of our control, but Ken was angry. He felt betrayed. It was against the Island way of doing things, based on trust.

I had to focus on getting them back on their feet and back into our supply chain. However, after the initial Canadian debacle and the latest events, our relationship with Paul was never the same.

While this was happening, I turned to our Sri Lankan supplier Kal, to back us up more. Our relationship had started at one of the food Expos in Sydney with a personal introduction via the Sri Lankan Consul.

Kal was selling dried tropical fruit and spices. At the time, I was looking to expand our range into other coconut-based foods, especially one of my favourite traditional Banaban foods – *ka maimai.* The fresh coconut sap was boiled until it turned into a sweet thick syrup.

The Banabans had used the syrup for centuries as their natural sweetener. While I had tried to assist them in developing this product, it was not possible at village level.

On the Island, men had the traditional daily role of gathering the sap while the women's role was to turn it into *ka maimai* for the household. I was amazed that Kal knew a man back in his community who upheld a similar tradition.

During the months that followed, we developed a working relationship with Kal, who happened to be a food chemist by profession. I described the products I wanted to create, and he knew how to work with his people back on his island to manufacture what we needed. I was excited about working with him, and after a year we went to Sri Lanka to see his new factory set up.

Sri Lanka has an excellent coconut industry which the government recognises as one of the country's primary export earners. Unlike the Pacific, the industry had generous support from their government and their focus up until that point had been on copra coconut oil, desiccated coconut, and coconut coir.

For our Australian market, these were basic lower-level products founded on high volumes and cheap pricing, utilising Sri Lanka's low manufacturing costs, especially when it came to wages.

Kal was so grateful we had taken him on board to work with us. Until our introduction, he had found the Australian market difficult to crack.

At the time in Australia, some Sri Lankan's immigrants were often, in a racist manner, viewed as either refugees or boat people. The stigma carried over in business. I liked Kal, his Buddhist values, his hard work ethic; to top it off, he was smart.

Sri Lanka is a beautiful country, and on our first visit, I saw how serious Kal was about building a new industry. More excitedly for me, he was already employing about 100 people. Instead of the high-end machinery we utilised, he used manpower.

He hired a lot of people to provide them with an income – all the values I admired and what our company and brand had been built on. However, there was one big difference between Sri Lanka and what we were doing. Working with us for just twelve months, Kal had acquired a million-dollar trading loans via Sri Lanka's Coconut Development Board.

He had already set up his first factory and had just purchased land to set up a new purpose-built factory that would see all his production carried out in-house, not contracted out.

While I was excited for him, it hit me hard that we had worked for ten years with no such support and had to rely on our banks and private funding at high interest rates for our trade finance.

Our limit was $250,000, nowhere near the million dollars he had access to. While we had opened the doors for him into the Australian market, we had just opened a Pandora's Box with that money behind him and such cheap wages and operational costs.

After our first trip to Sri Lanka and handling more bulk export orders, I started to include some bulk oil with our regular food shipments.

While the Vanuatu bulk supply had dried up, I decided to invest in a full container from Sri Lanka. The virgin coconut oil was a new market for them, in a country entrenched in copra oil production.

The first time they included some virgin coconut oil in our shipment, AQIS (Australian Quarantine Inspection Service) had insisted on testing the oil for erucic acid.

I found that unusual at the time, as we had imported thousands of litres of virgin coconut oil, and we had never been required to have this particular test before. Erucic acid is not found in coconut oil and is commonly found in seed or other vegetable oils.

The virgin coconut oil Kal had sent us passed testing with flying colours. He assured me that the quality of Sri Lankan virgin coconut oil had improved to meet our standards. I was happy with their recent samples and subsequent analysis results.

I proceeded with the US$90,000 order. By this stage, Australian AQIS had stopped testing our Sri Lankan shipments for erucic acid, and the container load of oil arrived and cleared customs with no worries. Everything had gone smoothly until I had a call from Ken in production to come down and see him.

The oil from the Sri Lankan shipment that had come in was not only dark in colour, but Ken was concerned about a band of sediment that looked nothing like the usual heavier coconut particles found in our Island oil. It was more like a thick white paste and smelled odd.

Alarm bells went off.

I got onto Kal to voice my concerns, and he immediately said that it should be fine. He assured me they had tested the oil in Sri Lanka and forwarded me a copy of the analysis results.

Meanwhile, I organised to have it tested again, this time at our food laboratory. It came back and passed all the usual microbe analysis. I didn't think to test it for erucic acid.

After further discussions with Ken, who was not happy, we decided the shipment would have to be assigned to the horse, pet, and body product markets we had.

It was a large chunk of our oil resource and finances. Because the oil had passed microbe testing, our Sri Lankan suppliers brushed it off. Ken and I had every right to be suspicious of what they had sent us and to put it mildly, we were not happy.

Some other incidents began happening with food products we imported from Sri Lanka. Our orders had increased, and Kal was busy rapidly expanding production at their end.

He kept offering to assist us by taking over our packaging from his end to help us cut our costs. But for some reason, I kept rejecting his offer with the old principle of "not putting all my eggs in one basket".

I wanted us to oversee what we were packaging and use the quality controls we had in place with our strict in-house HACCP food standard processes.

I had made one exception, tinned organic coconut milk and cream that we had introduced into our organic range. This product had to be canned to preserve it, and we allowed our labels to be printed in Sri Lanka.

As these new product lines took off, Kal announced that he was building his own cannery to save the cost on contract canning. He went on to advise us that his new plant was a four-million-dollar project. While we were supportive as always, I realised that he must have a lot of other business going on to warrant such a large investment.

At this stage, Kal had been in business and working with us for three years. He had built and set up four factories in Sri Lanka. On one of our trips, I noticed he was packing virgin coconut oil for one of Australia's major supermarket organic brands.

I appreciated he was upfront about it. So, now I realised his new cannery would be part of that supply channel as well. While we kept waiting for our coconut milk and cream order to arrive, we found our regular shipments were continually missing key products.

While this was not unusual, over the following twelve months, the stock we relied on from them was starting to run critically low and even run out altogether. Now I had unhappy customers wondering when their backorders were going to be filled.

For our distributors, working with retail stores holding our existing shelf space for our products was critical.

We were so relieved when our coconut milk and cream finally arrived after twelve-months of constant excuses. We quickly advised our distributors their stock had finally arrived, and they took pallet loads of stock to fill their shelves.

I also discovered that Kal had launched the same products under his brand into the major supermarket chains. That was okay. I understood he had a new cannery up and running and needed to find new markets. We had a different niche market.

But what was not okay was that the supermarkets sold their products at retail prices for the same cost I had paid to import directly from Sri Lanka. Not only that, but I had waited twelve months for it to arrive, which had nearly destroyed my existing market.

To add more insult, I had to pay additional import duty, shipping costs and clearance charges as well just to land it. I realised our relationship was not as good as I believed it was. Other events would occur over the coming days that well and truly burst my bubble.

As I dealt with these negative interludes that seemed part of running a big company, we were now two years into the Palace of Dreams, and 2016 began well.

I had been on the phone talking to Jone in Fiji. He excitedly told me that the plantation's 800,000 trees were heavily-laden with what he believed would be one of the farm's best bumper crops to date. I couldn't wait to fill our warehouse with our prized Fijian oil. We had just landed a full container containing 20,000 litres, and we had another container in Suva ready to board the next vessel arriving in port.

Jone had worked tirelessly on upgrading the farm's production and had just put the roof on the new manufacturing plant he was building. He had spent one million dollars on a new boiler he had specially designed and had made for them in the United Kingdom.

The farm had always prided itself on being run on steam power, and the new plant would also be innovative. But spending a million dollars on a boiler was a big commitment, and just the mention of the word, "boiler" gave me a chill, reminding me of the Vanuatuan debacle.

Sadly, all our plans were brought to a sudden halt. On Saturday morning, 20th February 2016, Tropical Cyclone

21. The impact of Tropical Cyclone Winston on the farm in Fiji was devastating. You need to learn to cope with whatever is thrown at you in life and business

Winston, the strongest cyclone ever recorded in the Southern Hemisphere, made landfall in Fiji. It carved a destructive path right through Jone's plantation and adjoining village. It came in fast and hard, with wind speeds reaching 298 km an hour.

While our company's supply had been affected by cyclone damage on the farm in 2010 with Cyclone Tomas, the impact of this one was just unbelievable.

Ironically, I was in our boardroom right in the middle of our annual organic and HACCP audit when the first photographs of the farm were sent to me. I went into shock, which was not helped when the stupid auditor, who had conducted audits on Jone's farm, casually stated, 'Oh, it will be okay, coconut trees are genetically made to withstand cyclones.'

What an idiot! He was lucky I didn't hit him. He had no idea how bad the situation was. I've seen many photographs of cyclone damage over the years, but these aerial images were unreal. I couldn't even recognise the plantation in the photos.

I had locals contacting me to confirm, 'Yes, it is the farm.' One photograph had a boat sitting next to a house with a missing roof. I had to keep looking before I suddenly realised that it was Jone's boat that was usually anchored offshore in front of his house. Now it was sitting high and dry inland, up against his half-roofless home.

Even Jone's late father's house, built to withstand cyclones, had lost part of its roof. My heart just broke, seeing everything flattened around them and the surrounding 800,000 coconut trees stripped bare and standing at all different angles.

The island's only airstrip had been badly damaged and was closed, but I immediately booked Ken on the next international flight to Fiji with his essential satellite phone. His mission was to try and get to the farm as soon as possible to help them.

Ken was lucky enough to get on to one of the first domestic flights after quick repairs were carried out on the devastated island's local airstrip. With the long windy coastal road to the plantation wiped out in certain areas, Ken hitched a ride with government officials.

He went as far as he could via road, then he spent hours hiking overland to try and get to the farm before nightfall. What he discovered on his overland journey was traumatic.

By the time he arrived at the farm on nightfall, he was greeted by the news that one of the women had been killed by a falling coconut tree. She had been running between buildings in the middle of the disaster. Not only were the workers' houses mostly gone, the main house and the old plant were also damaged. Some of the farm's cattle had been killed by either flying coconuts or falling coconut trees.

It was an absolute nightmare as everyone, including the cattle, tried to seek shelter. With the coconut trees so heavily laden with their bumper crop, the aftermath was even more devastating.

The wind gusts had twisted the tops of some of the heavily-laden trees until the top of the trees had snapped off. While coconut trees are naturally designed to withstand cyclonic winds by bending over and coming back up, these trees would never recover once the tops of trees were gone.

Ken spent his time purchasing as much essential food and organising as many ration packs as possible for the workers and their families. The farm's school had also been damaged, and Ken made sure he included school stationery and other items for the children.

The adjoining Fijian village had been virtually wiped out except for one church building with a cross on the roof that somehow had miraculously been left standing.

Australian military troops started arriving on Jone's plantation in helicopters. They used the farm as a staging point for aid drops throughout the devastated region. With Ken at the farm reporting on the situation, I kept asking myself, 'How will I manage this one?'

This cyclone recovery period wasn't going to be a quick or easy fix. From my satellite phone conversations with Jone, he estimated a twelve to eighteen months growing cycle was needed to bring the trees back to proper production. Meanwhile, the new processing plant would have to be put on hold while facing the mammoth task of rebuilding and getting houses back to a liveable condition.

Ken finally arrived back in Australia about ten days later with a full report and photographs.

I had to face reality and the facts ... our company was now in deep trouble.

I had been there before, and yes, we had gotten through it, but now there was so much more at stake for our company. I had been facing so many issues on all different fronts, it just seemed endless, and I was exhausted.

My emotions were shot and virtually non-existent. I was a walking functioning shell of a human being. Now, once again, I had to put all my efforts into how we were going to survive the next twelve months.

The only way I could survive was to compartmentalise my thinking. I couldn't focus on the bigger picture.

I set achievable goals and targets that got us through each month, one step at a time. I had to stay totally focused.

First, I had to get Vanuatu back on board as soon as possible. Next, I spoke with Kal, and he offered to help us out. I also knew that I couldn't delay. I had to look for other suppliers as well.

Unbelievably, with all this going on, another recurring issue had reared its ugly head – the dreaded bane of my life, accountant dilemma.

Our new accountant, No. 3, was about twelve months in and had offered important advice regarding financial planning and wealth management.

With the lack of advice in the past, I jumped at the chance to put more effort into this. The years of juggling finances and living on the edge were wearing thin.

Now with a large multi-million-dollar company to manage and so many of our family members working with us, I had liked the idea of setting up a trust to protect our family's interests. I wanted to incorporate our children's futures into the company for the years ahead.

Ken and I had realised we weren't getting any younger, and we had to seriously consider facing our retirement that was drawing closer.

What accountant No. 3 was proposing was rather complicated and costly. I initially agreed to set up the main trust while we went about our other everyday accounting processes.

As the end of the financial year loomed, accountant No. 3 arranged a meeting, which I assumed was an end of year review and plans for moving forward.

He arrived with a younger gentleman and mentioned he was his new partner. Immediately alarm bells started going off in my head. I had heard a similar story last time when Con had to take on a partner during his wife's illness.

As our meeting drew to a close, our accountant suddenly produced a stack of paperwork from his briefcase and piled it on the boardroom table in front of me. It included volumes of financial reports and all the paperwork for our newly formed trust. Having not had an update on the trust project over the past months, I assumed he had rushed it through in time for the new financial year.

As I was trying to absorb all this, he added that he was semi-retiring and moving to the country, but would still be working on our account. At my quizzical look, he quickly added he would still be involved as a consultant, but all our regular accounting would be handled with his new Gold Coast partner's firm.

It then became clear he had sold out. Yeah, yeah, yeah, here we go again.

By this stage, he must have clearly understood my body language as he took more paperwork out of his briefcase and sheepishly handed me his invoices. As I started to look at them, he quickly informed me that they had another appointment to go to.

After they left, I sat down with my office bookkeeper and Ken and went through the paperwork. I tallied the various invoices. They totalled just on $30,000. It was no wonder he had shot through as soon as he had handed them to me.

With all the new trust documents piled on the table, I was swimming in paperwork and feeling angry. We had just been passed on to another new accountant, without my knowledge or choosing. I had been well and truly played and totally blindsided.

I couldn't believe it! Why was it proving so difficult to find a genuine accountant who believed in what we were doing; not just see our company as the golden chalice to suck dry?

Grudgingly, I maintained the status quo and worked on establishing a new relationship with accountant No. 4, hoping he would provide the level of service we needed.

Ironically, Con was in the middle of his own problems. He was in the process of dissolving his relationship with his business partner, who had never lived up to expectations.

I had always enjoyed Con's sense of humour over the years, and one of my favourite requests to him was, 'Just make sure you keep me legal. I don't fancy the idea of jail.'

He always replied that he loved me but had no intentions of becoming my jail buddy. With all the money I was spending on the high-flying accountants, I would have preferred to have Con back looking after us and protecting my back.

Once again, our company's funding and cash flow had become an issue. With so much increased competition, our sales fell. Every major supermarket chain was packing its shelves with virgin coconut oil, mainly from Sri Lanka.

Kal, our colleague, whom we had assisted in entering the market, was now our competitor.

All the complaints from our stores about our lengthy backorder delays had not helped the situation. I put the nagging thought that maybe there was more to these delays than I had initially thought.

I hoped I wasn't being manipulated, and the supply hold-ups hadn't been intentional over the past twelve months.

I held discussions with accountant No. 4 to discuss various ideas for funding and the idea of bringing in another investor, or selling off part of the company and retaining a licensing agreement.

We had so many divisions of our business by this stage, Ken and I thought it would be advantageous to spend more time working with our communities around the Pacific and concentrating on supply.

I was constantly receiving enquiries from brokers to sell, and ironically, I was contacted by one young couple I liked. While our sales were down, which was understandable with all the supply problems we were having, we still had a $2.5 million turnover, but with nearly a million dollars drop in sales over the past twelve months, I had to do something.

I initially believed our sales would bounce back once supply problems were sorted. Many companies had introduced coconut oil into their ranges; even Aldi was on the coconut bandwagon, again via our Sri Lankan friend. I had to face the realisation that our beautiful and valuable virgin coconut oil was turning into a cheap commodity, and it was disheartening.

We were receiving more enquiries every day for bulk supplies, which would end up back in the market competing against us.

I lamented that at least with bulk supply, we still had our finger in the pie, but overall our previously lucrative margins were changing. Now was the time I had to stop and research more marketing and other options to turn our situation around.

While I was in the middle of discussions with accountant No. 4, asking his thoughts on finding new funding, I received a pop-up window on my computer screen offering me a PayPal loan. I had no idea what the offer involved, so I clicked the button, and before I knew it, I had an automated message telling me that our account had qualified for an $85,000 loan secured against future PayPal payments.

My account with PayPal had been operating since the early 1990s. I must have put a lot of money through PayPal over the years. All I had to do was work out the time period I needed the money for, and the interest rate automatically adjusted to suit. I chose two years for the loan period, just in case, and hit the submit button. Everything was approved in less than a minute, and the total amount was credited to our account within 24 hours.

It was unbelievable, and after years of sourcing funding, it was the easiest and most flexible finance I had ever received. Every time we had an online payment, a percentage was deducted from the amount to pay off the loan.

It was so effective that I paid it back within the year, which allowed us to use the option again, but I never took it up. Once again, things were about to change.

 **LIFE LESSON:** *Sometimes the universe has different plans for us. Things that are totally beyond our control.*

22. For Stacey, sailing her yacht and going to sea every weekend was her sanctuary away from the stress of business.

CHAPTER 9

HOLD ON TO THE DREAM

How do you hold on to your dream while everything seems to be going wrong around you? Not easy! I had to keep moving forward.

While I have mentioned all the problems that provided so many challenges, I realise I probably should have spent more time addressing issues; being tougher as we began to haemorrhage money on faulty stock or, in the Vanuatuan case, no stock!

I became an expert at juggling things in my head, but as all these negative issues were getting added to the mix, my mind frantically assessed the situations as they unfolded.

My focus was to keep driving the company, and more importantly, our work team forward. While there were good staff around me, the bottom line stopped with me. My relationship with my highly valued suppliers and growers was a personal one that only Ken and I could handle.

The first step was learning to become a scrooge, reassessing everything, including our overall spending. Our management team detailed our processes with a fine-tooth comb, and our purchasing tightened up. Nothing was purchased unless I double-checked each purchase order and signed off on it.

My staff were not used to me being such a scrooge, but it had to be done. Our profit margins were still good, but our monthly distribution orders had dropped.

We still had a high demand for bulk oil, but of course, some of the larger orders were going to our competitors.

My theory – right or wrong, was that it was better to have a bit of something than zero of nothing, or even worse, let someone else step in to fill the gap. But with the level of bulk customers we now had and the reduced supply, we had shifted to a higher-volume turnover with lower margins.

Some of the companies who had ordered a regular bulk supply from us for years were good payers, and I had allowed them to go on fourteen-day accounts.

I sent a letter to advise them that due to demand and the fact that we now had to fund and ship separate bulk shipments, all bulk orders would require a 50% payment at the time of order. The balance would need to be paid on arrival in Australia before delivery.

While they were initially taken aback by my new trading terms, I knew some of them had tried to import directly from our farms and cut us out of the picture.

If they were looking at bringing in and funding their own direct shipments, they could fund the special bulk shipments we were bringing in for them.

As the old saying goes, "out of every negative, there is a positive". Sometimes it is hard to see anything positive as you become absorbed in the negativity around you.

I received an invitation to attend a Pacific Coconut conference in Fiji, as one of their guest speakers. Even though it was not the best timing to head off for a week to Fiji, I took up the offer when I realised Terikano would be attending. She would be representing our Women's Village project with other coconut growers attending from around the Pacific.

The conference was all about supply chain, and to be surrounded by genuine and emerging coconut growers was what I needed to put things back into perspective. I put together a presentation on the Banaban story, from our humble beginnings to our state-of-the-art production facility at the Palace of Dreams.

I never realised how much my talk would inspire them all.

Ken was not in attendance, but they knew of him and that he was an Island boy from Rabi, and they related so much to our story and its humble beginnings. Terikano followed up with a presentation on the Island's Women's village project, and it was the perfect addition to everything we were doing and believed in.

I also met George, the young operations manager from the Fijian government-sponsored virgin coconut oil project up in the northern region of Fiji. The government had invested in new plant and machinery, and he was keen to find a market.

While they didn't have organic status like Jone's farm, they were processing coconuts from local Fijian growers throughout the northern region. The area was rich in naturally grown coconut palms. The trees throughout the area were well established, mature trees similar to those growing over on Jone's island nearby.

Our conversation was just what the doctor ordered.

Within days of getting back to Australia, George's sample arrived. The oil tasted and looked good, and the test results back from the lab supported the quality.

Of course, like all Fijian government-sponsored projects, they still had the mindset that manufacturers would make around wholesale and retail returns on their oil.

I had to give George a reality check, especially when their oil didn't have all the associated expenses involved with organic certification and levies.

We finally agreed on a price, and I assisted George to get the proper export packaging. Our new supply chain was nowhere near the capacity of Jone's farm.

However, with Jone still in cyclone recovery mode and the Fijian government backing this new processing facility, I knew we could help them expand it to meet our needs.

The spirits of Ken's ancestors were still there looking after us. Fiji had just come through for us and saved our bacon.

LIFE LESSON: *Remember, when you run accounts, you are not a bank. You are in business to make money, not finance someone else's.*

The Vultures are Circling

Our latest PayPal funding boost had really assisted us. However, I had an overwhelming feeling that the market was still changing. The days of creating a wonderful new market were over, and we were starting to swim in the lower end of the market, in the highly competitive grocery arena.

With bulk orders increasing every day and more coconut oil flooding the supermarket shelves, I sadly realised that Kal had done a great job of taking over the lower end of the market.

They were supplying and contract manufacturing for most of our competitors' brands appearing on the supermarket shelves. All the products were packed in Sri Lanka, not Australia, and with such low wages and costs they were able to drop their pricing to create a very cheap product. We still had a loyal customer base behind us, but there had been a shift.

Again, I realised it was time for us to look at various options, such as selling off the Australian side of our operation and our distribution channels. I had the idea of a licensing agreement and holding on to our export and supply chain channels.

The plan was to find a buyer with an existing business in the industry that would benefit from adding our product range and extensive distribution sales network to their business. Ideally, they would utilise our fantastic facility and staff. Ken and I could still be involved on the supply end.

We had a lot to offer the right investor, and I also had people, not only staff but thousands of farmers and villagers, relying on us. But in the end, the weight of the decisions sat heavily on my shoulders.

I couldn't sit back and wait for things to happen. As hard as it was, I had to be proactive, adjust, and broaden my thinking about the business.

Yes, things were changing. All businesses go through peaks and troughs. We had reached our critical mass years back. Now with the explosion of everything coconut, the money we had poured into research and marketing was only assisting everyone else to come on board and be part of the action.

I finally agreed to allow the young business brokers to put out the feelers and privately list our business. There was to be no advertising. The offering should be kept confidential until prospective buyers were adequately qualified, and I approved sharing our information. I didn't want our business and its figures to fall into the hands of our competitors.

Over the coming weeks, the brokers sent details to various companies showing interest. Most enquiries came from fellow manufacturers interstate. However, when I inquired further, most didn't have the sales channels or experience in marketing required to handle a company like ours. They were probably more interested in moving our facility interstate and getting hold of our customer base.

I not only had our staff to worry about but the future of supplying our loyal online customers.

This is where our business was unique. It covered various levels from bulk sales, manufacturing, wholesale, retail, online, and export.

While we had about ninety product lines on our books, we only had about a dozen core products. The rest were all the same, just packaged to target different markets such as health, food, organic, non-organic, body products, baby products, and pet products. There was not an ounce of wastage in our business. I had developed a market for all levels of our production.

I had also assisted our farm in Fiji by developing a value-added product – organic coconut crunch – a by-product of their unique processing method.

One day our brokers sent through an enquiry from an investment group based in Sydney which also had connections in Brisbane and the Gold Coast. The more I checked into their background, the more they appealed to me.

We set up various meetings, and their management team flew up from Sydney to meet us. When they walked through our doors and toured our facility and our large, fully stocked warehouse, they were impressed.

Apparently, they had visited a lot of businesses and manufacturers but could not get over the level and extent of cleanliness and organisation they witnessed at our facility. There was not one section of our building that wasn't kept spotless.

They seemed to be a young, dynamic team with various investments on the Gold Coast. David, their young Executive Director, also held a Chairman's role on the board of directors of one of Australia's major sporting bodies involved in the Olympic games.

He assured me they had an experienced team of people in their group. He stated they could help build our business further. One of their team had extensive experience in the supermarket supply chain throughout Australia and overseas.

Their ideals and experience seemed a great fit and what our company needed. It was agreed they'd put together an offer after their next board meeting.

The broker rang me about a week later, telling me they'd heard back from the group. She said their offer was not what we had expected and wasn't sure if we'd be interested.

Before they invested, they wanted to send in one of their colleagues based in Brisbane. He had a wealth of experience as a CEO in other companies they funded, mainly in the technology industry, and he'd be good at crunching our numbers.

They informed us our business was just below the group's net profit threshold they usually invested in. They talked about KPIs, and I explained that I knew the margins on all our products and margins weren't based on a set KPI but adjusted to suit the product and the market.

Typical of me, I was used to doing it my way, but they wanted to make sure our figures and margins were correct and viable before coming onboard.

They also needed to put together financials that would be suitable for the trade funding they worked with. I met their colleague, Vic, who seemed to know what he was talking about.

He mentioned another Brisbane-based colleague in their team, a so-called expert in online marketing who was keen to work with Brynley.

After discussions, it was agreed that Vic would be engaged on a three-month consultancy basis. This would give him time to assist us with our financial reports and prepare us for trade funding. Of course, he would not give his time for free, and I agreed to a monthly retainer of $3,500 and reimbursement of his travel expenses.

I thought this level of consultancy would be beneficial. It would be good to work with these people over the coming months, especially if they were going to invest in taking over our company.

The group had no intentions of working in the business except for appointing Vic as their CEO. It was imperative they maintain our workforce moving forward, and uphold the brand and our Company Mission to assist all our people back home.

Over the next three months, I worked extensively with Vic, dissecting everything. He had already highlighted some interesting points regarding our business that I had not been aware of.

He identified that I paid our accounts too quickly and that I should move all our payments to a monthly payment based on EOM 30 days.

He also suggested that his group could get better debtor and trade finance based on other companies they were already working with. The trade finance company they used would fund our imported stock based on a Bill of Lading as the ships left port from the various countries. Instead of the minimum six-week turnaround and longer when there were shipping delays, they'd finance our stock while it was still on the water. Their other division would then provide separate debtor finance based on our Australian sales.

Vic suggested more changes regarding our main coconut suppliers. When he saw the money that I had been paying them over the years, he could not understand why I hadn't asked for trading terms.

I had always worked on the principle that nothing left our factory unless it was paid for. While my suppliers were usually paid once the stock left port, in Sri Lanka's case I had to pay for the shipments in full before I could clear them in Brisbane and then take possession.

I started to get a clear picture of how these guys operated and how they funded it all. They used everyone else's money to finance their business, and I could see why they were in the investment game.

That was another reason they wanted to increase our profit levels, to cover the finance on the shipments, and still give them a good return on investment.

Everything made sense, and it wasn't the way I had operated. I had to look at the bigger picture, and I had to adapt and make the best decisions to benefit everyone who relied on me.

 **LIFE LESSON:** *Trade finance to fund your stock, debtor finance to provide cash flow, and your suppliers fund your operational costs?*

It's Lonely at the Top

I can look back now and see how all these situations and dynamics left our company vulnerable. I'm sure Ken and my stress levels didn't make it easy for our staff to work with us. As they say, "shit runs downhill ..." and not a more accurate statement is ever said.

We hit the marina in Brisbane every Friday night to Ken's credit, where our yacht was berthed, and returned late on Sunday nights. He loved being around people, whereas I needed peace and quiet on the boat to get my head together for the next week. The time stuck with me in the confines of a floating vessel must have been terribly boring for him. Thankfully, we both enjoyed fishing. Our yacht was the one thing keeping me sane.

I had to stop, shut my brain down and have a break. It was my survival mechanism. Ken and I had been together for nearly twenty years. We have been working together in the same business for the last twelve years, sharing Our Cause and dreams to make a difference. But I had to admit Ken's idea of handling stress was very different from mine. His first forty years spent living a laid-back Island lifestyle was at odds with the stress levels he experienced owning a multi-million-dollar business.

With my involvement at the high level of management, I have garnered a lot more respect for CEOs and the exorbitant wages they are paid to manage it all. There are few people you can talk to at this level of management. I'm sure if you were to ask CEOs the question, and they were honest enough to answer, they would agree that it is lonely at the top.

Who do you share your inner thoughts with? Who do you confide in? You cannot share your doubts with anyone, as it brings negative ideas into your thinking and even voicing them to yourself can let doubts start to creep in. For women, it is a role-reversal situation when we become the breadwinner. For me, it made me realise the level of responsibility men have carried over the years. Many of my younger female business colleagues may feel differently about this, but I grew up in a male-dominated professional and business environment.

Men went to work while their wives stayed home to rear the kids. The men came home to a cooked meal, kids washed and in bed, and they expected to be pampered.

After working with men over the years, I wonder how many of them had to compromise their work ethics to keep employed, staying in jobs they must have hated, to support their families.

While this situation has changed, I believe there is even more pressure on both parents to support their household. With the government's encouragement for women to return to the workforce as soon as possible, Australia is now relying more and more on childcare centres to raise our children. We've added more pressure to our relationships and our family life. I loved having my children growing up and working with us. Working with our family was one of the main highlights for me; regardless of it not being ideal for business reasons, it worked for us.

I think this is why at first, I enjoyed Vic's consultancy. He was someone to discuss business with and share the passion of growing the business and the problems we were facing in a changing market.

My relationship with Vic was professional. I did not discuss my personal feelings or my relationship with Ken. However, it got to the stage where it became evident that Ken and I were not in a good place.

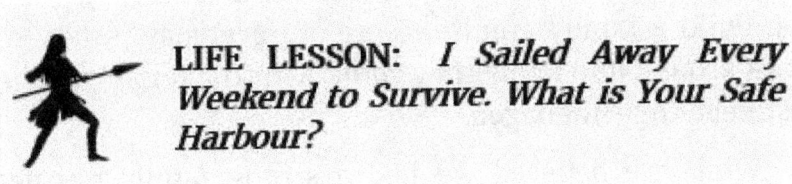

LIFE LESSON: *I Sailed Away Every Weekend to Survive. What is Your Safe Harbour?*

Family Business – the Bane of Investors

There are many lessons to be learnt in the period that started off so well and ended up six months later, becoming the fight of my life. How, you ask? How could such a situation evolve when you bring a paid consultant and a potential investor into your business?

How could everything suddenly turn so sinister and unbelievably challenging? How did everything Ken and I worked so hard for over the past twelve years come under threat?

To put it simply, a family business is the bane of investors! So, what do I mean by that statement?

A family business is a living thing involving family dynamics, personal relationships, sibling rivalry, and allowance for behaviours that would usually not be found or tolerated in the business sector.

These same behaviours can be a company's greatest strengths with strong bonds that make the business impregnable. It can also have the opposite effect by leaving the company vulnerable to unscrupulous attacks, using divide-and-conquer principles.

Investment groups see family dynamics as standing in the way of doing good business, especially when it comes to company profits. Of course, that makes sense, but when you build a family empire, there are everyday issues you work around and know they come with the territory. They just need to be managed.

While we believed we had a strong family business based on a dedicated Cause, the investment companies only focus on return on investment (ROI).

Interestingly, our investment group specialised in investing in family-owned businesses that were well established, successful and had been operating for years.

They looked for companies that were starting to become stressed, including principals nearing retirement age, sudden illness or death, or the businesses growing to a level that needed to look at restructuring to adapt to changing markets.

Except for illness and death, our family business ticked all their boxes, which was another reason I thought this group would be the perfect fit for us. How could I have gotten things so wrong?

I knew from the beginning that they were dissecting all the family dynamics within the business, assessing who they thought had potential and who didn't.

They were impressed with Brynley's online expertise and quickly introduced us to Robert, who had digital marketing experience in their group, hoping he could team up with Brynley.

Just as I realised the relationship with the investment group was potentially dangerous, a new problem arose in our family situation. It had been one of our greatest assets until this stage, but now it seemed like it was crumbling.

During past years, as more stress had entered the business, I made the hard decisions, usually on my own. Ken had his son, Kabuta, helping him in production, and as part of his traditional custom, this allowed Ken more time to step back and act in a management role rather than on the front line of production.

He taught Kabuta how to operate the machinery, and except for the odd problems when Ken had to step in and fix things, he let Kabuta run production.

Ken's role was setting up daily work rosters, sorting out any problems and making sure we had enough stock on our shelves in our warehouse.

The months of stock delays had caused a lot of tension between us. It was frustrating, but I was doing my best to rectify the supply problems.

After Ken's return from Fiji and the devastation caused by Cyclone Winston, his stress levels were even more elevated. He believed that now I had taken over as CEO, he had been pushed aside, which meant everything was my fault. Of course, this didn't assist me or the situation at hand.

On Ken's Island, he had a lot of responsibility with his cultural role as clan spokesman. In Australia, I had become the one in the business that people wanted to talk to.

Ken felt left out and naturally resentful. But his dented ego was the least of my worries as I worked even harder to hold everything together.

There were so many people relying on me, and Ken made sure I knew he was stepping back.

I felt more and more on my own.

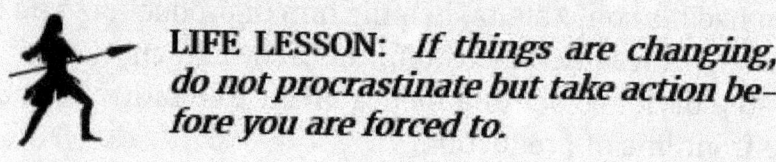

LIFE LESSON: *If things are changing, do not procrastinate but take action before you are forced to.*

The Vultures Have Landed

As Vic's three-month consultancy came to an end, we still needed more work to complete the business plan. I needed the plan to present to the investment group's board, and it would form the basis for the level of investment we needed. It was also required to enter into new trade financing arrangements.

For the final stages of the project, I extended Vic's contract on a monthly basis. Vic saw that our sales were down, but he was aware of our limited supply situation. He worked on budgets and forward projections based on increasing stock levels.

Meanwhile, I took Vic's advice and approached our coconut growers to assist us with trade terms to help us out.

Ken and I explained our new funding and investment plans to our growers, and to their credit and Vic's amazement, they came on board. It was at this time when Vic realised the strong bonds we had with our farmers and suppliers.

As we rolled on to the five-month consultancy period, I noticed Vic was setting up meetings with the people and companies his group worked with. He wanted us to change our accounting software.

I pointed out that this would be at an additional expense, especially when we needed our current program to manage our extensive inventory and in-house order processing, which was crucial to our daily operations.

Before I knew it, Vic was organising more meetings. He wanted to bring in various third-party providers for our general bookkeeping, payroll and even to manage our inventory.

I was keen to learn about all that was on offer and broaden my knowledge. Obviously, his overall plan was to reduce our administration staff as much as possible, having everything managed over the cloud. While I understood his motive, these changes wouldn't come cheaply.

Another proposed change was to bring in their highly recommended accounting firm. One look at our Profit &

Loss report and it was clear just how much money we were haemorrhaging with accountants' fees.

I was not that happy with accountant no. 4 and the way we had been manipulated. Vic had already asked him to present a written quotation for his services and charges we would require moving forward.

No more creative accounting fees.

Accountant no. 4 was not happy. I swear, asking him to provide us with a written quotation, was like some type of dirty word. He obviously felt challenged. His inherited nest egg was now under threat.

Rather than provide us with a written quote over email, he requested a meeting. He marched into our boardroom with his clerk in tow. I spent the next hour with him while he justified his services and levels of expertise.

Little did I realise he was also charging me for this meeting to do his pitch, and I was paying a high hourly rate for his underling to attend.

I had already made my mind up, no. 4 had to go, and while I was glad to see the last of them, the fight over the charges on his ridiculous final bill had just begun.

I moved quickly on engaging accountant no. 5, a large Brisbane-based firm the investment group worked with, to take on the cursed role, but soon warning bells sounded as Vic pushed to make even more changes.

It became evident that the group expected us to fund all the changes they wanted to implement before they came on board.

I slowed down, making more changes and keeping my own counsel to see how the game would play out. At the same time, I began stalling for time. I was developing a growing dislike for the way Vic spoke to people in meetings, and his demands.

Okay, you are saying, he was just being tough, a good business operator. The way he talked to people was very much at odds with how I treated people.

I began to look at Vic differently. My respect level was starting to shift, and I had this overwhelming negative impression that he was acting predatory. In fact, he began to resemble a bird of prey - a vulture, to be precise. From that point on, I couldn't shake the feeling.

Vic finally completed the business plan and presented his findings to me. Contrary to my thinking about the way the deal was going, he was genuinely taken with the fact that we had a darn good business, with decent margins after all.

I had tried to tell him that months ago. He stated we had too much debt, but with the proposed new trade funding levels tied in with debtor finance, we could build on everything from there.

He believed an investment of $300,000 was required, mainly focused on boosting our stock levels. He wanted to build our lucrative online channel even further by combining Robert's experience with Brynley's marketing skills.

One of the most significant changes we needed to implement for the new trade financing was to part ways with our local debtor finance company, Cash Resources. It had worked so well for us over the years. Unfortunately, even though they had expanded their financial services, they were not at the level yet to offer us the valuable trade funding we needed.

Meanwhile, the new finance company Vic proposed had much higher fees and a minimum $30,000 annual interest level for the debtor finance component of their funding.

Worst of all, it required us to sign a three-year contract. I had nothing like this with Cash Resources and was not happy.

In the end, I stood my ground and only committed to utilising the trade financing component from his suggested company. Taking on their costly debtor finance would've been a step backwards. Of course, Vic wasn't happy, but it was our business, and we were footing the bills.

Finally, Vic had no more excuses. Our new business plan, budgets, and forecast were ready to present to David's investment group. Now we just needed to see what offer the group would come up with.

As month six and December loomed ever closer, we waited. Due to my previous discussions with Vic, I believed an investment of $300,000 would be on the table, and I was keen to see what the rest of the offer would entail.

About a week before our proposed meeting with David's investment company, my intuition paid off when Brynley came up to our office and asked to have a private meeting with Ken and me. She seemed distressed when we sat down, so I asked what was wrong.

She told us that she had been invited to attend a private, confidential meeting with Robert in Brisbane. To her surprise, Vic was also at the meeting.

As usual, Vic took over proceedings from that point and advised her that they would put in an offer for our company. Brynley was well aware of Vic's involvement in our business over the past six months. It soon became apparent they wanted her to run the company for them.

Vic had picked up that Brynley had been feeling disgruntled with what we were paying her and thought she should be paid more. They wanted to take advantage of the situation. Initially, Brynley thought they might want to offer her a marketing job in one of their other ventures, not turn on her parents' own company!

What Vic didn't know was that Brynley wasn't comfortable in any management position. Over the years, she had been thrust into various roles to manage other staff, and she hated it. She loved working in a team environment and was even happier working on her own.

Brynley drove home after the meeting feeling stressed. While she had agreed to the confidentiality surrounding their discussion, she felt her loyalty to us was far more important. She had to tell us. There was no way she wanted to go behind our back and betray us.

The meeting was a high-risk move by the investment team and showed the level they were prepared to stoop. They had very different plans for us going on behind the scenes. Vic and Robert's involvement was far more than just your average consultancy. Our suspicions were well-founded when Ken overheard a phone conversation between Vic and one of their clients. Someone was yelling at him so loudly over the phone Ken could hear most of the conversation.

23. The company's production was specially designed by Ken.

When an ashen-faced Vic got off the phone, Ken asked him, 'Are you okay? That did not sound good'. Vic, caught off guard, mentioned that it was a family business with two brothers, and they were blaming him for the bank wanting to sell one of the brother's homes. Apparently, it had been used as collateral for their business.

When Ken relayed the story to me, I realised we were in a similar position. Ken said it was clear from what he overheard that the two brothers were at each other's throats. I also had heard snippets of other calls Vic had received over the past weeks. This family business had operated for around twenty years and was well-known on the Gold Coast.

All I kept thinking, was 'What have you done, Vic the Vulture, to these people?' You don't survive in a family business for twenty years without a working relationship. Two brothers being torn apart, resulting in one brother losing his home. Wow, alarm bells had turned into sirens, and their clandestine meeting with Brynley only consolidated our views.

Ken and I were even more convinced. They were not the people we wanted to take over our company, regardless of their investment offer.

The day finally came when David and the rest of the investment team arrived in our boardroom. With all that was going on behind the scenes, I asked Con to attend on a personal level. I not only valued his opinion but knew he had our backs. I also asked Helen, our inhouse legal advisor, to attend.

David was thrown off guard when he saw the team I had assembled. He immediately asked Con who he was, his professional background and his business interests.

Con cheekily answered that he was a personal friend with business experience and was only attending at my request. No wonder I loved Con so much; he kept a stern look on his face to match his vague reply.

They were all uncomfortable with Con's response. Vic the Vulture had never met Con or seen him in our office. He had no idea of his connection to us. They already knew of Helen's legal role within our company, but it was clear that Con's presence was worrying them. In fact, for the first time, David, the director, seemed rattled.

David began by telling us all the great things he thought we wanted to hear before adding that our business was stressed. Our company needed funding to survive and, more importantly, move forward. He stated they had the right people within their group to make a real difference and access new sales channels for us.

I don't know why, but from the moment he started to recite his well-rehearsed script, we knew we were being buttered up for "the offer".

The best was yet to come when he stated that their investment group really believed in Our Cause and what we were doing to support the "*Binna Burras*".

Ken and I looked at each other, trying to hold back the laughter.

Vic, his loyal vulture consultant, sat back, keeping his mouth shut for once. He realised David's mistake but was not prepared to correct him in front of everyone and interrupt his speech.

My mind was going one hundred miles an hour. How could these guys genuinely believe in our business when David didn't even know the name of the people or our brand name after working with us for six months?

Our Cause was the keystone of the business.

David looked so relieved when he handed the reins over to Vic the Vulture so he could put forward their investment offer.

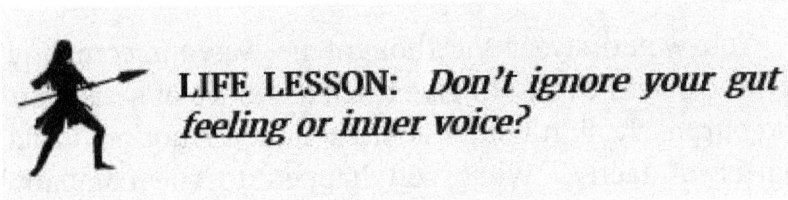

LIFE LESSON: *Don't ignore your gut feeling or inner voice.*

The Offer

Here we were, gathered around our boardroom table with David, the boss, and Robert, their Brisbane marketing man, both looking nervous. Of course, Vic was in his element, doing all the talking, as cocky as ever. Their body language said it all. They were so focused on their well-rehearsed spiel that Ken and I seemed incidental.

As the Vulture continued, all became clear. Ken and I would retire as directors, and they would take over the running of the company for the grand total of one dollar.

That was it!

So why a dollar, you ask? Technically a dollar is all that is required to make a contract legal. If they had offered $2, it would mean that they would have to prove that they could operate the business successfully enough to meet the company's operational commitments and pay down any outstanding debt. But at the time, we had no understanding of the significance of what it meant.

The big offer we had waited six months for and all the hours of work and additional funds I had outlaid to get us to this stage amounted to one dollar. No wonder they were so nervous except for the Vulture who sat there stone-faced.

You would swear Vic thought he was our company's saviour. I didn't want to give them an ounce of satisfaction and purposely didn't show any reaction or emotion. I asked matter-of-factly, 'What will happen to the company's debts?'

Vic calmly replied, 'The company's existing debts will be your responsibility and not part of the deal.'

I then asked, 'What's happened to the $300,000 investment we discussed?'

The Vulture replied, 'We need that money to fund the company moving forward.'

During my exchange with the Vulture, David had his head down, not wanting to look at us. I realised how weak he was. He had no heart and had to leave it to the Vulture to handle things when the situation got tough.

After a pause, gathering all my strength to sound as calm as possible, I said, 'So, what you are proposing is, to now walk in and take over our company for nothing? No talk of shareholding, licensing, profit share?'

The Vulture calmly repeated his mantra, 'No, we are offering one dollar.' David again squirmed silently in his chair.

Ken stepped into the discussions and asked, 'What happened to all your talk six months ago about opening up new sales channels you offered to assist us with?'

'Good on you, Ken,' I thought. Abruptly I smiled and stood up, bringing the meeting to a close. 'Thank you all for coming.' I added that now they had finally put their offer on the table, we would be pursuing other investment offers we were working on.

Again, their body language was priceless. They all looked to the Vulture for an explanation for what was happening.

Obviously, I had really thrown the cat amongst the pigeons. They believed they knew everything about our company. They wanted to continue discussions, and David suddenly found his voice. 'We can talk about some type of profit share.'

I ignored him and confidently smiled as I showed them to the door. They asked what other offers we had received. Ken interrupted again for the second time. 'You made it clear you had no intentions of investing in our business, so there is nothing more to discuss.'

Good on you, Ken!

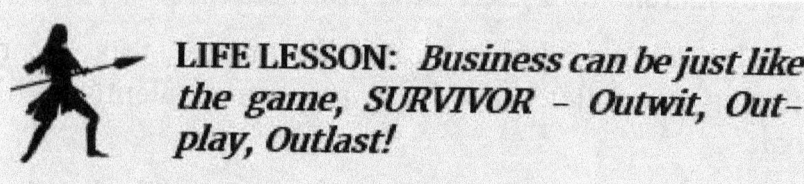

LIFE LESSON: *Business can be just like the game, SURVIVOR – Outwit, Outplay, Outlast!*

Heading into Battle

I always knew that anything in business is possible. With years of experience under my belt, this latest episode was a classic. What really got to me more than anything else was they thought Ken and I were stupid. Vic the Vulture had no idea that I had been holding my cards close to my chest, and thought I was an open book. He never knew I'd been having discussions about other investment options with other potential investors.

They were playing on our emotions and the passion we had for our family, our community, and Our Cause, painting our situation black, and they were there to rescue us. Really?

After receiving "The Offer", their overall strategy of how they intended to play us had become clear. String us along as long as possible, complete a comprehensive business plan with three-year forecasts, and make the necessary changes to run our business remotely with the least number of administration staff. Get rid of Ken and me and tell everyone we had retired although we were still consultants to the company.

The icing on the cake was to leave both of us with all the company debt, and more importantly, no way to service the debt. Oh, and not forgetting, before Ken and I exited the scene, we would have implemented all the new changes and additions they wanted. We would be paving the way for their takeover at our expense.

Retelling this event seems almost comical. I don't know anyone with a sound mind who would take up this offer. In fact, there was NO offer!

I soon found out they weren't prepared to walk away and let some other investors step in without a fight. They believed they were on the verge of swooping in and taking over our multi-million-dollar business for nothing. What sickened me even more was the realisation that they must have used this strategy before, and it had worked.

There was no way you could contrive a plan like that without knowing they had been able to pull it off before. Who were their last victims? Was it those poor brothers and their family business that sounded like it had been utterly shattered?

When their plans collapsed at our last meeting, they had to act fast and began working on Plan B. Ken was key to implementing their next move. I had allowed them into our inner sanctum and paid Vic just on $20,000 in consultancy fees. While I had initially enjoyed the process and ended up with a detailed business plan with projections for the next three years, I never realised how damaging the past six months had been in other ways.

The reality of the situation came to a head the day I returned from my trip from China. Our company had received an unexpected award from Alibaba as one of their

Top 101 International Sellers. With everything happening around me, I'd made an effort to accept the offer to attend the awards ceremony at the company's headquarters in Hangzhou. It was a fantastic trip and a great experience after all that had happened over the past twelve months. We'd all been through a lot, and a positive and uplifting trip to China was just what I needed.

Meanwhile, back home in Australia, Ken and other members of the team were being bombarded from all different angles. Introducing the investment team into the business had unsettled our staff and family.

Unbeknown to me, the company's woes were all being blamed on me. While we were still doing a $2.4 million turnover, we were hurting, and sales had dropped a million dollars over the past eighteen months.

Maybe I had taken too long to act and address the problem, but I still believed once our supply shortages were rectified, we would regain traction and bounce back, gaining new sales markets. I had already conducted a lot of research into launching a few of our products in the US via Amazon's online sales channel, especially with my new business contact in Spain who was experienced in this market.

With the current situation of reduced cash flow and strict budgetary measures, my risk-taking days were significantly reduced.

After sitting in on our meeting with the investment group, Helen, our inhouse legal consultant, took it upon herself to review the legal ramifications of trading insolvent. She mentioned having talks with someone she knew with experience in this area. We were still holding up, but we had to take on an investor, or we'd have to look at closing our company down.

I thought it was strange when Ken phoned me in China and mentioned Helen had asked him to meet up with her in Brisbane for a private meeting. I asked him why Helen would want to have a private meeting away from the office?

She was in the office a couple of days a week, so what was going on? What was so important that she needed to talk to Ken privately the moment I was out of the picture? Helen hadn't been happy during the past months over our prospective investment group's involvement, and it was made clear from the onset that they would not require her services if they came on board.

What I hadn't realised was that Ken was being bombarded with offers from Vic the Vulture. He knew I was away, and he was busy working on Ken, stirring him up over my management style.

He told Ken it was my fault the company wasn't doing well. They wanted to help him, as a fellow director, to save the business for his people. The Vulture worked hard on driving the wedge between us, and he knew Ken was stressed to the max over the whole issue.

They assured Ken that he had every right to take over control of the company as a fellow director. Unbeknownst to me, Ken had confided in Helen. She was also in Ken's ear, telling him not to do anything unless he spoke to her first.

Thank goodness she supported the fact that the investment group was trying to use him. But she also added that if Ken wanted to go down this route, she had people that could help him out. All this pressure was thrown at Ken while I was away, and I was oblivious to how far they were prepared to go to stab me in the back, to get what they wanted.

Our company was the prized jewel that these so-called experts wanted. To Ken's credit, he told them it would be my decision on the future of the company, and he wouldn't be signing any documents while I was away. But on a personal level, these latest episodes had driven a bigger wedge between us.

It wasn't until I arrived back from China that I had any idea of just how bad the situation was back in the office. The atmosphere seemed subdued when I came bounding through the front doors. I was keen to call a staff meeting to give my team a briefing on what had happened in China. I was shocked. China seemed to be the last thing the staff wanted to hear. Apparently, they had been told that the business was closing, and they should start looking for jobs elsewhere.

I was completely railroaded. Helen, my legal consultant, and so-called friend, who I had known back to my flower shop days, had also been stirring the pot. My staff briefing that had started so cheerfully downstairs had abruptly soured when one of my best staff members suddenly burst into tears and unexpectedly resigned.

Wow! What had just happened? What the hell was going on? As the situation and the level of discontent unfolded, I called Ken up to the privacy of my office.

Ken informed me about the level of unrest with the staff and, much more importantly, within our family. I was devastated! Not only had I been blindsided, but my heart was wounded.

Everything happening in the business was manageable and did not pierce my protective amour. But on a personal family level, it was very different.

I was so busy trying to save the company that I never realised how much damage the relevant stress was causing my family. My management style and personality was now the focus of their discontent. Various family members seemed to have lost faith in me and had already made plans to leave us and move on. Hearing this left me feeling shattered.

While we had outplayed our investors, or so I thought, we had lost the war. They had done an amazing job of destroying the essence of all we stood for – our family. It was only in recent times that I found out the level these investors stooped to. They did everything possible to try to convince Ken to turn against me and take over our company.

That was just their first step. They then wanted Ken to appoint another one of their colleagues as an administrator who would restructure the company and turn things around to make our company viable. They made it clear that Ken had every legal right to do this.

While they had done an excellent job of dividing our family and us, they underestimated Ken. Vic the Vulture sent Ken a text one morning just after my return from China with a proposed 10 am deadline. Their man was ready and waiting for Ken's instructions to take over the company.

They advised Ken that they had already made plans to have me escorted from the building. All those years of our hard work building our dream. Our shared passion for building an empire for our children and community, yet it had come to this.

Thank goodness Ken never allowed this to happen. We might have become estranged, and we were not getting on, and yes, he was blaming me for our current situation. Even with our family divided, he could not do that to me.

These people never realised the overall depth of our relationship, all we had achieved as a team over the years, and the undying passion we shared for the Banaban Cause. They tried to take advantage of two people whose personal and working relationship had become dysfunctional due to the immense stress.

It would take Ken more than a year after this event before he informed me of all the tactics Vic the Vulture and the investment team had tried to pull off. Meanwhile, unaware of all these other issues going on behind the scenes, I felt so alone. While various family members made plans to gather and celebrate upcoming Christmas celebrations, I couldn't be two-faced and pretend everything was okay. Thankfully, my invitation went astray in the mail.

Instead, I headed off to the safe sanctuary of our yacht and headed out to sea on my own.

Another more important matter in my life was unravelling behind the scenes during this time – my mother. The closest person in my life and my most trusted ally and pillar of unending support had been exhibiting unusual behaviour and was finally diagnosed with dementia. This was the one time when I needed her the most, and it was the first time in my life when she couldn't be there for me.

It also made me realise that I had to get my priorities right. My mother's situation was so critical that after a recent fall at home and subsequent hospitalisation, the doctors advised that it was no longer safe for her to live independently.

Thankfully, and to my brother Dan's credit, once he knew the pressure I was under at work, he and his wife Teri immediately took up the reins and moved my mother in with them in Brisbane. Ironically, Teri is also a Banaban and happens to be Ken's cousin. Without their support, I don't know what I would've done. Their assistance gave me such inner strength knowing that Mum was in a safe place with people who loved her. Even my days of taking her out with me on my yacht were over. It was too dangerous now, as her dementia deteriorated.

I safely tucked all these emotions away deep in my heart. Her unconditional love, her support and undying loyalty just reminded me more of just how much I missed her.

 **LIFE LESSON:** *At the first sign of weakness or when struggling to survive, the sharks will attack. Be prepared! Anything is possible!*

24. Stacey at Alibaba HQ China, making a presentation.

CHAPTER 10

WELCOME TO THE CUTTHROAT CORPORATE WORLD

The early months of 2017 flew by, mostly in damage control and adjusting to the loss of some of our key personnel. There was a lot of pressure on staff, knowing how much I was fighting to save our company. Overall, the remaining staff were loyal to the company and me. They also wanted to keep their jobs.

Meanwhile, I worked like a trojan with other possible investors, spending time in meetings and travelling interstate to talk with prospective investors.

With the levels of stress I was going through, especially personally, I shut down my feelings. Once again, I had become a highly functioning shell of a human being. I had to stay focused and not allow myself to feel.

I trusted no one, and sadly that even included Ken. But thankfully, I reached out to two of my very close business colleagues and personal friends. They were also going through similar downturns in their businesses. Greg had just taken on an investor, while Steward had been fighting major legal battles with his partners. We were all on the same wavelength, so I decided to open up to them and discuss what had been happening.

It was the best decision I ever made. They immediately stepped up to offer their support and share their own experiences, and more importantly, they had my back. They also knew what impact our working lives had on our relationships and families.

It was the first time in a long time that I knew I wasn't on my own. They both helped me keep up my resolve to fight, and not cave into the pressure. Hearing their stories and what they were going through gave me the strength to go on. Their words of encouragement and respect for me helped me tackle all the negativity around me.

Their opinions mattered, not the views of people with their own agendas.

Greg had taken on new overseas investment partners and arranged to set up meetings with his group. He believed our company could be a good fit for the broad health industry portfolio his investors were putting together. They were a large international investment group made up mostly of Asian investors, but managed by the corporate team based on the Gold Coast and Sydney.

Over the following months, I entered into a series of meetings with the group's team from different management levels. It was a long, extensive process as our company was dissected even further, and Ken and I were put through the wringer.

While my previous experience in the investment world had been very negative, this group was much larger with some impressive young corporate professionals.

Our final meeting was with James, the group's CEO, who was impressed with our company and our mission. He believed we would be a good fit for their group. They were prepared to invest and support our mission with the Banaban community.

We knew that with our lack of funds, we needed this deal to save our company and keep our dream alive. Our main concern was to get the investment we needed, protect the brand name on behalf of our community, keep our staff and jobs for all the hundreds of farmers we worked with.

Ken and I had both decided, moving forward, we wanted a percentage of the profits put in a trust for the Banaban community. We believed if everything went well, we would be retiring in the next few years, and we needed to ensure that the community would still benefit from what we had begun and not end up being exploited.

James and I discussed our shareholding expectations, level of investments and our exit plans based on Ken and I remaining with the company for at least the next three years. He made it clear that they would take over the majority shareholding on behalf of their investors.

He finally advised they would put together a proposal in the form of an MOU, Memorandum of Understanding, in the coming days.

LIFE LESSON: *A problem shared is a problem halved.*

When is an MOU Not an MOU?

While an MOU is usually a written agreement outlining mutually agreed terms to be included in a formal contract, it doesn't mean it's legally binding.

The investment group's MOU arrived the following week and was a beautifully crafted document focused on upholding our vision and Our Cause. The document confirmed their intentions to invest $850,000. Still, they needed Ken and me to stay on staff and run the business alongside their management team.

The main catch was that I would remain as one of the directors. Ken would resign his position but would still manage production. Due to the level of investment, our joint shareholding would be reduced to just 15%.

While the investment figure had already been discussed during our various meetings, Ken and I believed, saving the company and the Banaban brand for the community was more important.

The investors had agreed to allocate a 2% shareholding for a trust fund for the Banaban community, that Ken and I would administer.

As Ken and I went through the documents, tears welled in our eyes. After all the stress over the past twelve months, our company had been saved. But with all our overwhelming emotions, the heading on top of the document hadn't gone unnoticed.

It stated that the MOU wasn't a binding contract. We both eagerly signed the document and returned it with the understanding that they would take over the company on the 1st of July in time to begin the financial year.

With great relief, Shane, the group's COO (Chief Operations Officer), had been assigned to work with us and as our company's new managing director for the next three months. He arrived at our office with John, our newly appointed CFO (Company Finance Officer).

John was also assigned the other key role as a fellow director on our newly formed board. The hard work began while we waited to sign off on the formal contract, which the group's in-house legal counsel was preparing.

We had just entered a new world with a team of professionals in the fields of finance, management, and legal, and a division specialising in immigration law and investment. We now had a plethora of corporate experts around us. Except for Shane, our COO, no one else on their staff had hands-on business or marketing experience.

They seemed more than happy to let Ken and me run the show. Still, I knew the executive team had their eyes on Brynley, but a key element of the MOU was that Brynley would remain for two years heading our company's marketing team.

Her marketing role was vital to keep growing our lucrative online markets, especially with our plans to launch online in the US.

Shane was a good guy who also held the same role in my business friend, Greg's group of companies. With Shane's new position with us, he had to manage three companies located 120 km apart. He was so overwhelmed with the workload he would leave us to manage on our own, after a twice-weekly rushed management meeting.

My focus was on building up stock levels as soon as possible and implementing a solid marketing campaign strategy. But there was a major hold up.

No funding could be released to us until the contract was signed. I never realised this would be such a long and tedious process, and it took another six weeks before four contracts arrived. Each document averaged about 150 pages and was a minefield of legal jargon.

Once our lawyer studied the documents, it was confirmed we were signing our lives away. Compared to the wording on the MOU, the only mention of the Banabans was that their 2% allotment would come out of our 15% shareholding.

Shareholding wise, Ken and I knew we were screwed. We still had our management roles and existing salaries, and all our staff retained. All our debts would be paid up.

Tutu, our Banaban daughter-in-law and Ken's son, Kabuta, who were working for the company on a 457 work visa, still had their jobs to remain in the country.

Ken and I thought it was a sneaky move to take the 2% for the Banaban trust fund out of our meagre shareholding. Still, if losing another 2% meant protecting and establishing a trust for the community, it was worth it.

By the time the contracts were signed and the money finally hit our account, the new stock didn't arrive until the end of September. These further delays meant we had drawn down on all our stock reserves and were critically close to running on empty.

Another critical issue arose that we hadn't expected. James, the group's CEO, asked Brynley to work out of the group's head office while waiting on our stock to arrive. He wanted Brynley's skills for the group's upcoming international conference.

While Brynley wasn't that excited about it, her focus was on our brand. She wasn't able to say no. We believed it would be a good experience for her to work in the corporate sector and broaden her skills. It was a different work environment compared to her life, growing up in our family business. Once she moved to the main office, she loved the people she was working with but became quickly disillusioned by the corporate world. It was not for her. Her heart was focused on saving our brand.

It also became apparent that James might be the CEO of an international investment group, but he had no understanding of Brynley's role in our business. He just knew she was smart and wanted her to weave her magic to market his corporation. In fact, the entire management team had no idea of what eCommerce involved and how much online marketing contributed to boosting sales.

For our company, this was when we needed Brynley to hit our marketing hard. We were now three months down the track, and we finally had the funding and the stock we needed.

The new age for the Banaban brand was ready to go.

LIFE LESSON: *Forget all the fancy titles. They do not guarantee the person has the ability or knowledge to live up to the title.*

Board Meetings from Hell

Ken and I embraced the changes and adjusted to the new chain of command and the corporate way of managing things. All our new colleagues seemed to have fancy titles, and now there were three of us at the company's helm. All of us had to report back and answer to James, the corporation's CEO, at the monthly board meeting.

Ken and I happily and confidently walked in to attend our first board meeting about six weeks in. All the executive team were there, and at this stage, we were still waiting on our contract.

It was good to catch up with Shane, our elusive COO and touch base with John, our new CFO. But the moment James, the CEO, arrived to chair the meeting, the mood changed.

Tension filled the air. As James's voice boomed, he asked for progress reports from our newly appointed executive team. I saw them visibly sink back further into their chairs.

This was the first time I witnessed these usually confident men appearing nervous and their words so measured. It was a whole new world for me.

I was used to saying it as it was, with no fear or concern of being challenged or shot down in flames. In this new corporate environment, it appeared that the main objective was to fly under the radar. Keep your thoughts to yourself and only provide answers to direct questions and nothing else.

What a lot of crap!

How could you run a business if everyone ducked for cover and turned into "yes men"?

Obviously, the most important goal was to keep our CEO happy. But it soon became apparent that James was displeased when he found out Ken and I had not received our contract.

This meant the delay in funding our new stock supply. He reminded Shane that he only had three months to get everything up and running and six months to get our business turned around. I naively tried to point out that stock would not leave our suppliers until we had the money to pay for it. We had to allow at least another six to eight weeks for stock to land and turned into finished products.

I left the meeting feeling sorry for Shane. He'd been put under the pump, and obviously, in this world, there was no room for excuses. This meeting would only be the first of many. Poor Shane only lasted three months and left just as our stock finally arrived.

Now we were assigned one of the corporation's big guns, Winston, who happened to be the COO for the group's Sydney office. He not only was appointed as our new COO but took over the role as managing director now Shane had departed the scene.

I wasn't sure how they expected this to work, with Winston living in Sydney. He was a real show pony, and overly confident, highly aggressive business-wise, and his management style was built on intimidation. Winston took delight in pointing out your weaknesses and was light on praise. I soon discovered his views of his own abilities were not shared with all the executive team or staff behind the scenes.

Office politics was alive and blooming in the corporate world.

With all this in mind, I didn't care. I was only interested in working with him and the task at hand. Winston never originally intimated me, but he lived up to his reputation during board meetings that followed.

There is one thing I don't tolerate, and that is being spoken to like I am an idiot. I don't care who you are. It's not on.

During the board meeting, we butted heads over the fact that I needed money allocated to implement marketing. Winston's immediate response was, 'Until you make money, you cannot afford marketing!'

I knew then that I was going to have to work with my hands tied behind my back. While Winston believed he knew everything, he had no concept of marketing. I also found out during the meeting that the group was in private negotiations behind my back with one of our competitors, that had set up operations nearby. They were minor players in the industry but copied everything we did, especially when it came to our online sales channel.

I had known Harry, the company's founder, for years when we worked together while I was consulting for a natural health company. He was a naturopath and used his title to make health claims.

Of course, the suits back in head office were impressed with Harry's title. They believed that they could utilise Harry's supply chain by investing in his company, and combine his business distribution with ours.

While, in principle, it sounded good, his supply was out of his connections in India. Australian consumers found it hard to trust the quality of Indian-produced coconut products.

In the new age of virgin coconut oil manufacturing India, unlike the island nation of Sri Lanka, was not considered a serious supply source on the global stage. As the procurement team conducted the round of meetings that we had also gone through, I was confident they would never pull off a deal.

I knew our investment group would never pay Harry's over-inflated asking price with their much smaller business operations. Meanwhile, my friend Greg was already having problems with our investment group. They had acquired his group of companies about six months before us. He was on the phone lamenting that his business had become a revolving door of operation managers (COO) they had brought in. Now he had the group's Malaysian investors sending their staff over to take up key positions.

Greg's investment structure was different from ours. We shared the same Malaysian investor who owned a chain of natural health food stores. On paper and in theory, we were all a good match and shared similar synergy. Greg was a reputable and long-standing natural health professional.

He had developed a good relationship with our Malaysian investors, whereas we seemed to have been kept in the dark. We had never had the chance to meet them personally.

While I felt it rather strange, I knew how busy they were, and I kept focused on the tasks at hand. But by November, the reason behind this became apparent.

 **LIFE LESSON:** *Board meetings – listen carefully and assess the play. Know when to speak up and be prepared to be shot down in flames.*

When Enough – Is Enough

I worked so hard to get us back on target. With Winston the Show Pony, everything had to run past him. When you consider how I had spent the last thirteen years not answering to anyone, I believed I was doing a pretty good job of slotting in generally to the corporate chain of command.

Okay, I still occasionally shot my mouth off at our company's monthly meetings, but generally, I learnt quickly how to play the game.

While the Show Pony loved to strut his stuff, prancing all around our whiteboard, I just shut down. It was always about crunching numbers. I had learned to not even mention the filthy M (marketing) word. I would've been given a far better reception if I dropped the F-bomb.

For the first time in my life, I hated attending our monthly meetings. Sadly, they weren't a place to share innovative ideas or thoughts. I was disengaged in the whole process, and I preferred to say nothing, know nothing, and not give a hoot.

As Winston put all his stuff over the whiteboard, he apparently, decided that I was to come up with a sales plan.

He wanted me to get on the phone or knock on my customers' doors and get sales on the board.

His words piqued my interest. So, what was he suggesting? Apparently, I was going from company founder, managing director, CEO, and current director to a sales rep.?

I hadn't had contact with our stores since we began back in the late 2000s, and most of our stores would be through our distributors. I knew all the leading players, but he wanted me out of the office every day pounding the pavement.

For goodness' sake!

I let it all wash over my head until he kept addressing me for a response, and boy, oh boy, I well and truly got his attention.

I casually replied, 'That is what my distributors do with their team of sales reps.! I can't just walk into my distributors' stores and go over the top of them.'

I could not help myself when I said, 'It just doesn't work that way!'

Winston had never thought of that. He had no idea how the distribution side of the business worked. The big man of the finance world was an absolute numb ... numb.

With him not wanting to lose face, of course, he added, 'Well, do up a sales plan and present it to me.'

Again, I was on a roll and could not help myself. 'What's that?'

Well, that evoked a response, and I didn't give a stuff. I thought he might explode.

25. Stacey catching up with Terikano at Fiji Coconut conference.

'What do you mean? Are you telling me you don't even know what a sales plan is?'

As calmly and as nonchalantly as I could, I replied, 'No, that's what I paid my marketing and sales team to do.'

The look on his face was absolutely priceless. I know, playing the fool is not a role I would typically relish, but the devil in me was unleashed. 'Don't worry, Winston; I will just Goggle it!'

By the time he left the office, not happy, I ignored his instruction. I wiped off all the notes on the whiteboard, accidentally of course.

Over the following days, I became the topic of discussion at HQ. He instructed our CFO and his clerk to make sure they came into the office every day to see that I followed his instructions and got it done. Whenever one of them came in, I was too busy with clients or negotiating a supply deal. The poor clerk who was terrified of losing his job must have been copping it from Winston.

If they dared even mention the subject, I said, 'Yes, I'm working on it, but I am busy with other clients at the moment. I will get on to it as soon as I can.' Then I completely ignore them.

I had more important deals to pull off and get actual sales on the board, not this corporate crap. I had done enough reports, plans, budgets, and forecasts. I was over it. Can you stop talking about it and let me do my bloody work? I had put together an excel spreadsheet of clients I was currently working with on supply contracts. It involved a lot of work, and the costings and margins were all different depending on each deal. I had no intentions of handing it over to Winston yet.

He could wait. I wasn't going to jump at his command. Everyone else in their organisation might be scared of him, but I wasn't!

With Brynley tied up over at HQ and the loss of my other main marketing person, I was busy preparing for a one-day corporate supply trade show; to meet and pitch to the food buyers for the up-and-coming Commonwealth Games. Ken and I had to do this one on our own.

Like all these events, you just don't rock up on the day. Much effort needs to go into preparations, including display, which products you'll promote, bulk pricing, leaflets and samples for the buyers.

I was exhausted but pushed on. By the day of the event, it was one of those typically hot Queensland summer days. With so many people crammed into the hotel's ballroom, the air-conditioning was struggling. Other exhibitors resorted to opening all the doors to try and get some air in.

It was good to catch-up with fellow manufacturers and people we had known for years. At one stage, I caught up with a colleague I hadn't seen for some time. Suddenly, I felt strange. I quickly excused myself and rushed back to our display table, where I called out to Ken that I had to go.

Before I knew it, I was headed out the doors walking towards the garden. I didn't wait for Ken; my instincts told me I had to get out of there. Luckily, Ken must have seen the look on my face and had followed me outside. He caught up with me as I collapsed.

From what he told me, I had stopped breathing, and he was hitting my back to get me to respond. All I remember is being in an ambulance then the hospital. I was so out of it, I couldn't speak.

The rest of the day was spent having tests to ensure I wasn't having a heart attack or stroke. I finally came around and was deemed okay to go home. Apparently, I had just blacked out.

It was one way to make a dramatic exit at the event. Everyone was sure I'd suffered a heart attack. I had to take the next day off as I still wasn't feeling my old self. I went back to work the following day. I had physically pushed myself beyond my limits. It was like my whole body had shut down. One thing about my little episode was that Winston backed off and seemed generally more considerate over our Zoom calls.

I used the opportunity to let him know that I had follow-up meetings over the next week. I reminded him that I was due to fly to Melbourne as a guest speaker at an FMCG (Fast-moving Consumer Goods) conference the following Thursday.

The organisers had heard me speak at one of the various Melbourne Alibaba presentations and were impressed by our company's story. Winston had initially agreed for me to attend as long as it didn't cost the company anything. He obviously had forgotten all about it and challenged me about why I was going.

I played up the fact that I'd be able to tell them about his group's involvement with our company and our plans to start a Banaban Foundation. He liked that and gave his blessing for me to go.

I didn't have the heart to tell him; I didn't give a toss what he thought. I was only telling him as a courtesy, and

I wasn't a bloody school kid. I would have gone anyway, regardless of what he said. He added that I should try and pick up some orders while I was down there. He was so far out of his depth; he probably had no understanding of what FMCG even meant.

I put together a great PowerPoint presentation for the conference and flew down the night before. The night spent in a nearby hotel was a moment of respite from some of the pressure going on back home.

I got up early the following day, put on my face paint, and gathered every ounce of positivity I could muster.

The show had to go on.

LIFE LESSON: *Showing emotion in the corporate world is a sign of weakness. It's all about facts, figures and data. Nothing else matters.*

Broken Promises

There seemed to be a higher level of activity with the group's executive team than usual. Through the grapevine, I heard that our Malaysian investors had been staying on the Gold Coast for the past month.

One day John, our CFO, turned up at our office unexpectedly with a young Asian man. John introduced him as Kelvin, the husband and partner of our Malaysian investor. We were delighted to meet him finally, and Ken took him on a tour of our facility.

It soon became apparent, with Ken and Kelvin's cultural backgrounds, they got on very well. I couldn't believe it when Kelvin waited for John to leave before telling us that he and his wife had only just found out they were our company's principal shareholders.

Now everything made sense and why we hadn't met before now. Kelvin told us not to worry, and he was impressed with our business. Still, they had quite a few issues to address with the investment group managing their funds in Australia. Ken and I told him that we were keen to work with them and prove they had made a good investment.

We never realised that the investment group had deliberately kept us under wraps. However, the relationship between these two parties was not good, and little did we realise how much it would impact us.

Apparently, the group's $850,000 investment would finish at the end of December, and we were just beginning December. It had taken until the end of September to receive our stock finally. That had given us only October and November to bring our sales turnover back up to $150,000 a month. This was the first step in rebuilding our sales back to a healthy $300,000 a month.

We were slightly under our monthly target, and I was worried about December. It was always our worst trading month, as companies and businesses shut down for the Christmas break. Historically, October had been a strong sales month as our stockists built up stock for December trading.

Brynley had been working her butt off over at the corporate office. In her spare time, she had rebuilt our website to launch by December. To her credit, she had stood up to Winston. She challenged him that she could that she could rebuild our online sales to a level to turn our business around and boost our profit margins.

Meanwhile, I was busy bringing on new suppliers out of the Philippines, for our food production. I had already boosted our Australian bulk sales with new customers coming on board. Winston liked the bulk sales division of our business. While it worked on much lower margins, it was a quick way to build turnover with the least expense. Our overseas sales were still holding up, but I wanted them to get behind my idea to release a range in the United States via Amazon distribution.

I had involved Shane, our first Chief Operations Officer, in the various meetings with the Amazon consultants I wanted to work with. But after his short tenure, I had to get Winston on board, and he wanted more assurances on the return on investment. All the research and market analysis I had carried out with the help of a consultant looked promising. However, I couldn't give Winston a one hundred percent guarantee on projected sales until I tested the market.

I had just hit another brick wall. Winston dismissed the idea and wasn't even prepared to assign some existing stock and minimal funding towards a small trial.

Another episode in December made me realise that maybe our investment group had more going on behind the scenes than Ken and I had realised. I had been having a series of meetings about launching our brand in China via the daigou market based out of Sydney. I knew the young, dynamic Australian team behind this specialised group.

Knowing that Winston wasn't prepared to put any money into marketing, I had to think of other ways to enter this lucrative market. I already had been working on this distribution deal for almost a year.

So, I tried to stay positive and not waste an ounce of my energy on Winston's negativity. If I pulled it off and had a deal on the table, he would have no excuses to knock it back. I worked hard with the young Sydney team, negotiating agreed terms between us. They would be paid a percentage on all products sold. If their marketing didn't work, there'd be no commission.

If our sales took off in China, we all stood to do very well out of it. I was so proud of myself because there would be no upfront marketing fees. I put hours into preparing new product catalogues and new price lists to allocate the agreed sales commissions.

Within days, the marketing group rang me to let me know they had acquired a supply contract with one of the large online Chinese retailers who wanted our brand. Of course, I was excited and knew this was just what our business needed to boost our sales figures and get us back on target. They had already informed me the group's first order would be around $30,000 to test the Chinese market. They emailed through a contact for signing before the close of the day.

Now I had a contract I just had to get Winston to sign off and rang him before emailing it to him. I always tried to curb my enthusiasm when I spoke to him, but I admit I was excited. I had worked so darn hard to get this deal over the line, and I hoped once our stock hit the company's Sydney daigou store, it would be the first of many. If the daigous liked your products, the marketing was all word-of-mouth from that point forward.

The contract was a precise, three-page document with everything set out. There were no hidden clauses that I could find. I knew Winston would go through the document with a fine-toothed comb before forwarding it to our group's legal eagle and putting his signature on it. But I was not prepared for the video call that followed.

He questioned me on every negative point he could come up with. I happily replied that all these details had been negotiated to a flat rate sales percentage: no advertising or marketing fees, no monthly base rates, no storage fees, no nothing.

I quickly fired back responses and had answers to all his questions. I had seen how he operated and been on the receiving end to know I needed to cover all bases. I was so proud of myself for being able to negotiate this deal. I had kept both sides happy with one hand twisted behind my back and a negative Winston at the helm.

We concluded our conversation with him stating before he signed off on the contract, he wanted to meet with the team in Sydney in person. Of course, with him being Sydney-based, I thought he just wanted to take over the whole deal and big-note himself to James, our CEO.

There was no way his ego would allow me to get any credit for this deal. It was how these guys operated. There had been a lot of talk on his part and very little action until this point.

With all this in mind and the fact that he realised I had pulled off everything without any injection of funds, I patiently waited for him to sign the deal.

Winston rang me two weeks later to report the outcome of their meet up and signing of the contract down in Sydney. As I eagerly waited to hear details of our commencement date, Winston announced that he had asked them to put the deal and signing of the contract on hold until after Christmas. He told them that they were in the middle of restructuring the company for the coming year.

What the ... ????

Here I was working hard to set up this fantastic deal, and now this. What the hell was going on?

How did I feel? Devastated!

My enthusiasm went from one hundred percent to zero. As the alarm bells screamed in my head, I had that horrible sinking feeling that they did not want our company to succeed. Stalling on a hard-earned Chinese online contract focused at the daigou market, with the first order of over $30,000, and he wanted to wait until after the Christmas holidays. To add further insult, we had the stock now sitting in our warehouse. I felt like a fool after so much time and effort.

The young Sydney team had flown up to our office numerous times to work through the details. While Ken and I had become aware that there were issues between our Malaysian investors and our investment group, it left me questioning what they were planning for us behind the scenes?

I gathered all my strength to turn my focus back on what Brynley had been working on. She had done a fantastic job on upgrading our website and sales for December, based on just three weeks of trading, doubled to over $50,000. She was on cloud nine, knowing that all her strategies had kicked in, and proudly produced her figures at our next board meeting.

Again, Winston lived up to his reputation. He shot her down, stating that he believed the sales were only elevated due to Christmas sales and were no indication of a genuine lift in the sales figures.

This statement showed his ignorance. We had achieved these figures with no advertising or paid marketing, just Brynley's skills, yet he refused to acknowledge it.

By this stage, Brynley realised she was wasting her time. She had enough of trying to work with these people who had no idea of marketing or eCommerce. She resigned, deciding it was the time to go out on her own, and assured me that she would continue to help us build our online sales behind the scenes.

Again, I had to ask myself, 'What the hell was really going on with these people?'

LIFE LESSON: *In the corporate world, if you are not performing as per expectations, the slightest issue can get you into trouble.*

Breaking Point

The answers to my question finally became apparent in early February. While we had worked through Christmas to keep our sales going online, the group's corporate staff and management team had enjoyed a month off.

On their return, I was informed that one of their key people, Andre, who was a successful international investment banker, was coming over from South Africa to conduct training workshops with us. We had met him back in August when the group had held a three-day investment conference, and he had been one of the guest speakers.

Ken and I had also been guest speakers at the event. I had done a presentation on how Our Cause to help Ken's community had led to the development of our *Banaban* brand and business.

Andre was a personal friend and colleague of James, our corporation's founder and CEO. Andre made his money in merchant banking, and had walked away after a major health scare. His passion was now in helping others in health and community-based aid projects that he ran as part of our corporation's operations in South Africa.

Ken and I, of course, welcomed his input and assistance, knowing his background. He was more in tune with our corporate vision, or so we thought.

I tried to stay hopeful on the Chinese deal, but now Winston offered a new excuse that he wanted to hold off until after completing the upcoming workshop.

Meanwhile, I had been asked numerous times to attend a local business breakfast as their guest speaker. I had kept putting it off with so much going on, but I had run out of excuses, especially now the Christmas holidays were over.

The show had to go on.

I put on a brave face, calling on all my inner strength and dug deep to find my old positive self. Luckily, I had my PowerPoint presentation from my previous trip to Melbourne.

I was so close to becoming the "walking dead" by this stage. It took every ounce of strength to pitch our story and, more importantly, Our Cause to a lovely, dedicated group of fellow businesspeople.

This last presentation, for me, was like holding on to a glimmer of hope. It was probably good for my soul, but in my heart, I knew that our world had changed.

There was so much riding on Andre's upcoming workshop that James, our CEO, had arranged. Every time I asked questions, I was assured Andre's workshops were inspiring and just what all of us, including our staff, needed.

Andre finally arrived with his son, and virtually all work, except the bare essential online sales, was ceased. All our staff, about twenty-eight in number, including Karmeille, our dedicated and loyal cleaner, who everyone affectionately referred to as Mumma Bear, was made to attend.

We spent the next two days being told how wonderful we were and how Our Cause was the most important aspect of our company. By the first day, Andre had everyone in tears.

After all the pressure everyone had been under, that wasn't hard. Andre focused his talk mainly to our Banaban Islander staff, who had grown up with their history's struggle and injustice.

Like us, Andre said he understood the importance of family business and told us how proud he was to have his son work with him. But he also made it clear that our company would have to make money for future plans to work. Meanwhile, two of my managerial staff rolled their eyes at me. Obviously, not convinced.

By the end of Andre's non-stop workshop, I realised what they'd been planning for our business. They were going to turn us into an international charitable foundation set up for the Banaban community.

This was the dream Ken and I had always planned, and one we could still carry out in the years ahead in our retirement. Ken was very excited about helping his people, it was music to his ears, but I was far more sceptical.

I felt it sounded too good to be true. My once trusting and positive nature had already been well and truly tested to breaking point.

This saga's next step was a private session for Ken and me with Andre and his son. The executive group, including the invincible Winston, for once were strangely missing.

Now the depths of what was being planned behind the scenes was made clear. Therefore, it was important for Andre, to step in and handle us for this crucial step.

Ken and I were also a vital part of this. Unlike our previous dealing with Vic the Vulture and his group, they needed Ken and me to stay on and run it for the investment group's plans to succeed.

Andre's spiel kicked into high gear as he dazzled us with all his drawings on the whiteboard. I knew that there had been a lot of thought and planning behind this move.

Andre's tone and presentation were welcoming and music to our ears.

Still, when I raised questions or asked for more clarity, I noticed his demeanour changed from a caring humanitarian to a tough businessman.

I kept reminding myself; he hadn't made all his so-called millions in the banking world being a humanitarian. In the investment banking world where Andre came from, it was as cutthroat as it gets.

Just because he had faced death and had turned his life around didn't mean he had changed when it came to making money.

I also kept reminding myself, there was no way they'd have paid to bring him and his son over from South Africa for two weeks unless he offered a good return on investment.

 **LIFE LESSON:** *Never kid yourself. In the corporate world, it will always be about return on investment!*

CHAPTER 11

THE NEW VISION

The two-day workshop had been more about conditioning us for the changes the investment group planned to make. Ken and I were key to this move, so we had to be on board for it to work. Not our staff.

We were told that our product range would be reduced to just five of our highest selling products over the next six months. These products would be outsourced and contract manufactured to make our company more viable.

In other words, the end of our manufacturing and staff.

A charitable foundation would be set up with Ken and me running it, targeting international funding from government and major aid organisations.

For some reason, Andre was already envisaging a solar power project being set up back on our Island in Fiji as the first project. I thought it was strange when he hadn't been there and had no understanding of their needs. Clearly, he had experience back in South Africa in this regard and knew where he could get his hands on the funding for it.

When I raised the question about our staff, our facility and Ken's family here on a 457 visa, his demeanour completely changed. He quickly dismissed the topic to concentrate on the much bigger picture. He added that he'd be happy if we just reduced our range to only one product in the end. One product that we could utilise to get the message out there about Ken's people. Andre brought the meeting to a close and appeared happy with himself.

Ken and I were sent off to consider their plans, while I was asked to identify the five main products as soon as possible.

How can I ever put into words how it feels to cut out products that took years to develop and, more importantly, products our customers loved and supported. Now I understood why they didn't want us signing supply contracts or building our online sales and why our launch in the US was never going to happen.

They wanted it all gone.

Fourteen years wiped out, and all our amazing staff were going to become the casualty in their plans. Going forward, they needed just Ken and me and Penny, my personal assistant. Poor Penny's face turned ashen when I confided in her. She was expected to run the whole operation behind the scenes.

LIFE LESSON: *It is much easier to scale up your business, but far more difficult when you have to scale it down.*

What the New Vision Really Meant

Our company, as we knew it, would be gone. I knew in my heart there was no way our company could survive on just five products. We had so much competition that we needed a marketing budget to boost our online sales.

Brynley had already proven what growth potential we still had in our online channels. We knew we were on a winner with our new website and marketing program.

All we needed was a $2,000 monthly marketing budget to keep expanding our online sales; that would have us meeting our targets. We needed the products that the Chinese group had identified for their sales channel. We needed to invest in a trial for the United States with the Amazon channel. Without that, we were done.

I now knew the investment group had no intention of letting any of this happen. We would become a charitable foundation with plans to raise millions via Andre's contacts in the international aid sector. Ken and I would be working out of the group's main Gold Coast office. We'd be expected to fundraise, public speak, and strut our stuff to evoke sympathy using Ken's people as the bait.

Ken would be expected to stand up at their planned events and talk from his heart about his people, which usually brought tears to your eyes. Meanwhile, I would be busy doing all the business side of things; fundraising, proposal writing, planning, and coordinating projects.

Sadly, the writing was on the wall. We now knew why James was so keen to acquire our company for his group. It was not the business or even the brand they were after.

It was OUR STORY.

With their corporate connections in the international investment world, we would bring in millions, but in the end, what would Ken's people ever see out of all this?

For all the personal problems Ken and I had endured over the past eighteen months, we were totally united when it came to his people, the Banabans. There was NO way we were going to let Ken's people be used and exploited again. Especially using us and all we stood for to do it.

Over the next week, as everything sunk in, I stalled on the devastating task of reducing our product range that had taken years to build.

Winston phoned me to say that he would be flying up from Sydney to see me the following day to review and update progress after the workshop. He advised that he had meetings in the head office first. He turned up at my office around 2 pm, again with one of the finance clerks in tow.

He casually informed me that he was here to tell the staff they were being let go. He wanted to do the right thing and speak to them in person, not just hand them a written termination letter.

Apparently, from what I know now, the best time to sack or terminate your staff is at the end of the day, just before they are due to go home. You virtually tell them not to come back while they're in a state of shock. Just shuffle them out the door with their letter in hand before they get a chance to think about it, or God forbid, object, have a meltdown or ask, 'Why?'

This was a well-developed strategy, and because Winston knew most of our production staff were casual, he believed there was no need for seven days' notice.

Ken and I knew from Andre's meetings that they had planned this to happen in about six months. It was only last week we had Andre telling my staff how wonderful they were. We couldn't believe it. No sooner had Andre left the country to fly back to South Africa, everything had changed again.

Andre was due to come back in about six weeks to start working with Ken and me on the new foundation. I had already heard through the management pipeline that Andre disliked Winston intensely. Due to his relationship with James, Andre would be returning to take over the management of the whole group.

With Winston standing in my office telling me to call all the staff together so he could address them, I started to argue. I insisted he couldn't do that to our staff as many of them had worked with us for years. I asked what had happened to the six months we had been told? He coldly advised me there had been a change of plans.

I told him flat-out that I refused as a fellow director to be involved. Since he was the managing director of our company, he would be setting himself up for legal action. I believed what he was doing was unlawful. If he proceeded, I would be giving him a letter in writing supporting my claims.

I knew the keywords to throw at him. After all, he only cared about himself and making sure he was not legally liable. I also knew he hated things at the board level being put into writing, so I persisted with my argument. I was never going to stop him. As the managing director, he overrode me. In the end, I told him I'd only agree if he paid all the casuals an additional week's pay. He was furious about that, but I didn't care. I stood firm.

Winston reluctantly agreed. He instructed his poor offsider, who had been present, to draft termination letters for all my staff except for Penny, my assistant, who they deemed key to the business.

Helen, my legal consultant, who had her own agenda, had already had discussions with Winston. She convinced him she could offer legal advice far cheaper for them on her retainer than their legal eagle back in head office.

He agreed when she accepted a reduction on her retainer to stay on. Ken was advised he would be expected to run production on his own. Winston would only permit him to bring in casual staff to help him if he gave approval.

I also pointed out that Ken's family were employed by the company on a 457 visa and were currently awaiting their application for permanent residency. They needed time for the approval to be finalised. I pleaded their case, pointing out their son was finishing his final senior year at high school. If they terminated them, they would be legally required to leave the country within 28 days.

I finally negotiated that our daughter-in-law would stay on staff and work in lieu of her accumulated leave they needed to pay her. While it was not ideal, it kept them in the country and gave her time to get their residency through by staying employed by the company. If they lost their jobs now, there was no hope.

It was interesting that Winston, the Show Pony, when it came to the crunch, made me, as his fellow director, sign all the termination letters. It convinced me how weak he was. All talk and strutting about, but when it came to the hard stuff or putting his signature to it, he was gutless.

What he never realised at the time was that I left the letter for our daughter-in-law aside. In fact, I hid it. There was no way I was signing it.

I didn't trust a word coming out of Winston's mouth, and once my signature hit that letter, her employment contract would be over. Winston knew our production staff finished around four o'clock. By two-thirty, he called a full staff meeting gathering everyone around the downstairs office.

Winston announced that all the staff were being terminated. His minion meekly handed each of them their letter. He then spouted off that while the company had no obligations to the casual staff, the company would generously pay them an additional week's pay to help tide them over while they looked for a new job.

What a sad and traumatic day.

Winston had achieved his mission and executed it quickly, and except for our fight in the office, no one had time to react.

We were so shell-shocked as our minds tried to cope with what was happening around us.

No words can adequately describe how it felt; seeing people we cared for, who had worked with us for years, who had been an integral part of our dream, our vision, and considered part of our extended family, walking out our doors for the very last time.

Turning up at our beautiful facility the next day to see our production area shut down and so many desks in our office empty is when the full impact of what happened the day earlier hit home.

Over the coming weeks, I tried to rally us together and recover from the devastation. I kept stalling on the five products, and our distributors also thought the idea was ridiculous, especially with such good sales turnover.

We had plenty of stock, and sales had been good for the start of the year. We kept working with our skeleton staff to assist with orders coming in.

One of them was my young niece, Uma, who was nineteen, which meant she wasn't on an adult wage rate. She was preparing to go to university. It was so good to have her with me.

Tutu, our daughter-in-law, was trying to put on a brave face as she tackled more emergency meetings with her immigration lawyer.

Penny was my rock as always, but she had started to look for another job. How could I blame her? There was no way she wanted to stay on and work with these people whatever happened.

Winston and his crew were too self-absorbed even to realise that Penny was not on the Winston wagon. Of course, she got the first job she applied for.

Penny was an absolute gem, and I gave her a well-deserved personal reference. The day she finally walked out our door, I felt like my right arm had just been cut off.

Ken had already called on his son to help him out after getting approval from the powers that be.

The poor finance clerk who had got to know all of us rather well over the past months returned every day. He seemed highly embarrassed and sad at what had gone down, and obviously, he was no fan of the Show Pony.

He was also on a work visa with the investment group and had come from South Africa with his young family. He had a lot at stake. But while we liked him and sympathised about his position, his loyalty would have to remain with the group. So, we knew that everything we did would be reported back to head office.

Besides these facts, he seemed to have a good relationship with Andre, who had phoned him from South Africa to ask how we were all travelling with the new plans after he left? He was shocked and angry when he heard that Winston had intervened and terminated most of our staff the week after leaving.

Apparently, he had also asked the question, 'What happened to the six months?'

There were so much going on behind the scenes at the corporate level. The group's board was already making plans for Andre to migrate to Australia to take over the whole running of the corporation so James, the founder, could step back and retire.

But now, with what had happened with us, there was even more conflict going on behind the scenes.

I would have liked to be a fly on the wall during those frenzied meetings.

 **LIFE LESSON:** *Never ever give up. While there is life, there is still hope!*

Bring on Safe Harbour – Like Hell!

Over the following weeks, I heard Andre had arrived back in the country to take up the role as the group's new CEO. We were left mainly on our own, too busy trying to survive.

My fellow director, Winston, the Show Pony, had made it clear: there was no further funding available after I paid out nearly $100,000 for the latest container of oil that had just arrived.

Winston mentioned that they were looking at putting our company through a new Federal government restructuring process called "Safe Harbour". He told me that this would protect us, as directors, to bring in outside assistance to help us trade out of our situation.

I started my own research on what this new Australian government legislation involved. I had no faith in anything Winston told me now. Apparently, the legislation assists company directors to restructure their business and removes personal liability for directors to lead to a better outcome, other than liquidation or administration.

They had just implemented "Safe Harbour" for Greg, my business colleague's major distributor company, and I rang him to see what was going on.

He was full of praise and told me that he had a female accountant to assist his company with the "Safe harbour" process, and he was pleased about it. Greg was forever the optimist, and I knew he was being set up.

I tried to warn him, but he could not see the bigger picture. He was such a kind-hearted and genuine man, and I knew he was being played.

I had become increasingly hostile. After what had happened with our staff and blocking us from making new sales contracts, the writing was on the wall. Our days were numbered, and Winston's talk of "Safe Harbour" was just another way to manipulate and justify what was really being planned behind the scenes. It was also their way to bring in a third party to take over the running of our company.

There was no way Ken and I wanted anything to do with these people or let them get their hands on our story. They could plan and scheme all they wanted; we would not be part of it. We knew they didn't want our company. They wanted our story, with Ken and I to be their front for their much bigger plans of raising millions.

Word had already filtered through that the group's immigration division had allegedly overstepped the mark with immigration laws and lost major overseas investment. There was so much going on behind the scenes with these people, which was worrying.

The last straw was an email I received late at night from Winston. Short and sweet, to the point, he advised that he had resigned from his position as the managing director of our company.

So much for all his talk about "Safe Harbour", he was abandoning ship, and I knew that all hell was about to break loose. Like the Show Pony Winston was, it was all about him and protecting himself and his reputation. I had just been left as the fall guy.

Like hell I was?

They wanted to leave me as the sole director of the company and still control me.

26. There was only one Safe Harbour for Stacey, and it was not the one the corporate investors were peddling.

No ... way!

They had just relinquished their rights when Winston resigned, and they didn't appoint anyone else to take over his directorship. My legal eagle had already voiced concern over the various breaches in legal company procedures she had witnessed over the past months.

They might have been an international investment group, but their grasp on some aspects of commercial law seemed lacking, especially when it came to detail.

The next morning, I took on the real battle. Our last hoorah ... and all gloves were off. Ken and I had nothing to lose now. At the same time that this was unfolding, Ken's son and daughter-in-law had just received the devastating news from immigration that their application to remain in Australia had been rejected. So now it was all systems go!

The first step was to block the group's access to our company's main bank trading account. They had never added their names to our operational bank account even though they had taken total control of the finances since taking over.

This was also another grey area regarding the way they operated. As the sole director and only signatory on the account, I changed the passwords. I stopped answering their phone calls and emails. I started a series of letters questioning and challenging their legal rights over what they were doing.

We knew that the group's main Malaysian investor, and more importantly, our company's major shareholder, was also hostile and challenging the group's handling of their multi-million-dollar investment.

It convinced me I needed to see written proof that our investment group really did have the legal rights to represent our investor in their dealings with us.

Meanwhile, the group's newly appointed "Safe Harbour'" accountant or whatever title she came with, was the same one my good friend and colleague, Greg, had thought was so wonderful. She was now writing to tell me she had been instructed to commence work on a specific date to put our company under "Safe Harbour".

I wrote back advising her that as the managing and sole director of the company, I was not authorising her work with our company.

My actions took them completely off guard, and over the weeks and months that followed, I was able to block their every move.

Finally, the official replies from the investment group's legal department to our written correspondence threatened everything they could do to scare me. I still stood firm.

I knew from years of experience that this was a typical threatening lawyer's tactic. When you don't cave into their threats and legal jargon, they don't know what to do. I wasn't going to sit back and go down without a fight, and Ken stood with me one hundred percent.

Meanwhile, Greg was now on the phone in the final death throes of the "Safe Harbour" process. The same lovely lady he spoke so fondly of was now appointed as administrator to wind up his large distribution company.

Steward, my other close business colleague, had gone up to Greg's warehouse to check on him and found him there all on his own with no staff in sight. In his late sixties, he was left on his own to clear out his warehouse. After twenty years of trading, Greg's company had been reduced to this.

Steward couldn't believe the investment group had left Greg like this, too lousy even to pay staff to assist him. Steward took off his coat, rolled up his sleeves to give him a hand and help him through one of the most challenging times in his life.

This was the reality of what was behind their "Safe Harbour" strategy and what they had planned for us.

It only made me more determined than ever. Ken and I were not going to be used to do their dirty work.

 **LIFE LESSON:** *When you are in the fight of your life, you have to be brave and do what it takes to follow through. It's not about talk ... it's about action!*

Oh Bill, Oh Bill, Where Art Thou Bill?

In the middle of this battle, I received a phone call out of the blue. It was Bill, a good friend of ours we hadn't seen in ages. He was a private detective who also specialised in debt recovery.

He was a straight shooter and familiar with the corporate realm of banks, lawyers, accountants, and all the usual crap that went with it. He had been part of that world and knew what was behind all the jargon. As he stated, 'It was all just fancy bull ... to screw people over.'

He had no knowledge of what was going on, but he'd driven past our building and felt compelled to contact me.

Thank you, universe! He was just the man I needed to talk to. Even before I had a chance to tell him what was going on, he said, 'You know if you need help with anything or anyone, I am here for you. Just let me know.'

Before I knew it, I had Bill in my office assessing our situation. I gave him a briefing and showed him some of the dubious documents and subsequent correspondence.

He calmly turned to me and said, 'Mate, you are f***ked!'

Thanks Bill! Hearing that from him gave me the absolute clarity I needed; no more bull, fancy talk, or legal letters. After my continued challenges over their actions' legalities, the group finally produced a power of attorney with their hostile investor's scanned signature on it.

When I showed this to Bill, he believed it was probably a forgery, and my surviving in-house legal eagle wanted to keep going down the legal route. Don't forget her job was on the line, and while she was still employed, she now believed we had evidence they were acting unlawfully.

Bill immediately offered to mount a full-blown fraud investigation for me, and I told him to go for it.

A few months earlier, Ken had met Frank, a Gold Coast lawyer. Frank acted for a business group that came to visit our factory, with the idea of taking over our lease. I had already left for the day, and Ken had waited back for them.

Ken had immediately started an ongoing friendship with Frank, who was taken with the *Banaban* brand name and the history of Ken's people behind it. He also knew all the players in the investment group through his business channels. Frank became aware of the legal, contractual discrepancies we were fighting.

Frank was a decent man and offered to negotiate a deal to bring the matter to a halt and then to see us get a proper settlement to walk away. He believed with the money behind the finance group and all the other problems they were facing, they didn't need any other issues to add to their corporate woes. He believed it was a matter that could easily be negotiated and finalised.

Ah! I loved Frank's genuine enthusiasm and decided to engage his professional services, but I didn't share his confidence.

The end of the financial year was looming, and Frank was busy setting up meetings with the group's principal, who was just about to retire.

Meanwhile, our good friend Bill was busy stirring up the pot at his end. He had no faith in our new lawyer friend Frank, even with all his connections.

He had already investigated the main players behind our investment group, and his verdict was grim. Bill gave me advice on the best way to handle the situation, and he had me prepared for anything they would throw at me next.

I felt like a street fighter when I spoke to Bill, but boy oh boy, he was just what I needed. Bill had me down in the trenches fighting, while Frank, who was totally at odds with Bill's advice, took on the group the more acceptable legal way.

Frank reported back after each of his meetings, confident the negotiations were going our way. But I thought it was odd that the principal was not in attendance and had his son in a negotiator role. I believed his son was the least capable person for this role, while Frank was quite impressed by the young man and his handling of the matter.

Frank was on a high when he phoned me late on Friday afternoon. After the day's meeting, he was confident he would have the final agreement signed and in his hand on Monday. I tried to sound enthusiastic, but I just couldn't shake the sense of foreboding. I had already used all the money in our bank account to pay all our local suppliers and bring them right up to date.

I moved money for our superannuation into our holding account. There was over $400,000 worth of material and finished products sitting in our warehouse.

Most of our state-of-the-art machinery was nearly paid off, and our two company vehicles were paid off. Our rent was paid, and a security deposit was sitting in the bank to cover the lease.

Monday rolled around, and Frank's final meeting was held in his office late in the day, just before the close of business at 5 pm. We were already at home when he phoned. Just from the tone of his voice, I knew it hadn't gone well. He relayed the situation and what had evolved.

The meeting had already been delayed and started late. At the very end of the discussions, the son had told Frank that their finance group had already acted by contacting the bank to advise them of their intentions to call in the company's debt. Obviously, their "Safe Harbour" lady had good connections at our bank.

The son told Frank that the bank had agreed to put our account on hold. I immediately checked our bank account while Frank waited on the phone and was devastated to see all our business accounts frozen.

I got off the phone and tried to phone the bank. I ended up talking to people in the Melbourne office who informed me the bank had been advised our company was being liquidated.

What???

I tried to argue that as the managing director of the company, I had no plans to liquidate our company.

Whatever connections the group had pulled behind the scenes, my bank, who had been with us for the past twenty years, ignored me.

The bank had just become our enemy.

My next call was Bill. He quickly briefed me, and within half an hour, Ken and I had the family mobilised, and we met up at our factory for the final time.

With our operational accounts frozen and suddenly discovering that our company would be liquidated from under us, Bill advised that I immediately should resign as Director and walk away.

It had come to an end so abruptly, and we were all in shock. But I spent my final hours in our beautiful office surrounded by my family, the people that mattered the most.

They were there from the beginning and all so invested in everything this building and business stood for.

27. After fourteen wonderful years, our corporate investors decided to wipe the company out

It was important that they were also there at the end. Just like being surrounded on your deathbed with the people you cherish the most. They provided me with the perspective of what was important in my life. We had given it everything we had, and now it was over.

With Bill's assurance and not having any faith in the legal system and all the fancy corporate talk, Bill was the only person I trusted and was prepared to listen to.

Over the coming days, and with all the threats they threw at me, I was guided by Bill. He took over the dealings with the administrator and the bank. He managed the minefield of correspondence and phone calls through the process.

He kept enforcing his mantra to me, 'Doing nothing is doing something.'

Every business needs a Bill!

Had I stayed behind, I would have only assisted the Administrator in selling off our company to the highest bidders. There was a plethora of those wanting to get hold of our brand name and our 24,000-customer database.

Thankfully, with Bill looking after us, this didn't happen. Our Banaban Facebook business page had over 100,000 followers that could not be touched.

As Bill correctly predicted, the Administrator the investment group had appointed, quickly liquidated the company and sold off everything for just a fraction of its worth. The funds raised went straight into their coffers, and most of it was absorbed as their management fee.

I was so grateful that Bill had saved me from being involved in the heart-wrenching final winding up of our beloved business.

At the same, the investment group was in far more trouble than we ever could have imagined. Within months they closed their fancy office on the Gold Coast and laid off all their staff.

But like all experienced corporations with their network and numerous holding companies, overseas investments, and relevant tax havens, I am sure they will spring up again.

Due to all that had happened with the investment group, the Malaysian investor then appointed their own accountant to look after their affairs in Australia. He was a fellow countryman living in Brisbane.

Through Bill's assistance, we were asked to attend discussions with him on the idea of relaunching the Banaban brand.

During the meeting, he made it clear that the Malaysian investor had tried to stop the investment company's actions in putting our company into administration. However, once the administrator was appointed to our company, the investor lost control and was told they could put in an offer to buy back our company.

When the investor's company CEO back in Malaysia heard this, he thought it was ridiculous when they technically owned our company.

During our meeting, I voiced my concerns about the investment group producing a power of attorney supposedly signed by their Malaysian owner.

My question caught the accountant off guard, but he quickly replied that he was sure the owner would have signed it. He had just endorsed our suspicions.

He made it clear that their company had no interest in the continued support of the Banabans or Our Cause. They just wanted our brand to add to their portfolio for a public float they were preparing to launch on the US stock exchange.

There was no way we were prepared to relaunch our brand with these people either.

All Ken and I knew was whatever the real story was regarding the dispute between these two corporate groups, our beloved business had been destroyed in the process.

For us, the fight was finally over.

LIFE LESSON: *The best advice I was ever given, "Doing nothing is doing something."*

28. Stacey and Ken in their garden at home when the business began in 2004.

CHAPTER 12

GAUGING SUCCESS: WHAT DOES IT ALL MEAN?

I know I am repeating myself, but how often do we hear these supposed words of wisdom in business, "it's not personal, it's only business"? How many young up-and-emerging businesswomen and men add this to their daily mantra?

I was also guilty of embracing this mantra. It is a concept required in business to keep us focused on conducting business, making the tough decisions that need to be made that can affect people around us. More importantly, assist us in managing staff. However, this mantra also can allow the use of questionable or near-criminal behaviour to be committed in the pursuit of doing "good business"?

Why in business is this ideal so embraced and encouraged to become a successful business leader? Over the past forty-five years, I have found some of my colleagues and associates capable of some of the most abhorrent behaviour imaginable. Technically in some cases, it is the closest we can get to destroying someone and get away with it legally and even end up being congratulated for a job well done in the process.

Is this how you want to become known as a respected businessperson in your career? Is this how you want to live your life or the example you set for your children?

For me growing up with such a trusting and happy nature, I was totally unaware and unprepared for the extent people were capable of stooping to in their pursuit of success. I have experienced so much in my career, and when I was younger, it wounded me gravely. It hurt my soul, my being, as I wondered why people would do these terrible things. It also had me doubting myself.

Why was I so trusting of people? Why was treating people the way I wished to be treated myself considered a sign of weakness. Yes, I had to learn to toughen up over the years but still uphold my moral compass. Years later, when I took on the new battle of managing a multi-million-dollar company, I faced new business adversaries at a much different corporate level. It took all my inner strength to take them all on. To stand up on my own, listening and learning from the experiences all around me.

I didn't care if people with their own agendas assumed I was gullible or naive. It was good to watch them reveal their true intentions and allowed me to ask the questions to evoke their responses. I finally laughed to myself as they all thought I was clueless about what was going on. I even had one of my closest work colleagues tell people behind my back that I was difficult to work with, but she knew how to handle me to get what they wanted.

For women in business, some can get labelled a bitch or being known as difficult if they stand their ground and uphold their beliefs. While a man in the same position, taking the same stance would be judged as being tough but fair. I cannot tell you the number of times I have heard these statements. Why are women not given the same respect as being tough but fair? As the old saying goes, strength must come from within.

When people asked me, 'Did I have any regrets?', I replied, 'I regretted nothing in my life except for one thing, my loss over the years of trust in people.' More than regret, it was a feeling of overwhelming sadness of losing the love I had for everyone and everything in life. I had never wanted to look for the worst in people. But I had to admit I felt my rose-coloured glasses had been well and truly worn out and battered around the edges.

I still hold the belief that anything in life is possible.

However, now I am aware of the people around me and their "hidden agendas". I have learnt to hold my cards close to my chest. I was always such an open book. I still deeply care about other people. My trusting nature was a weakness in business, but it is who I am.

All through my personal and business life, I have never wanted to hurt another living soul. I am sure that I have, but it was never intentional. I could never live with my conscience for all the money in the world if I had to hurt others to get what I wanted or to get ahead.

In today's business world, the pressure is on to succeed at any cost. You need to question your motives and the reasons behind your decisions. You will have to make the tough judgements in your business that are going to impact the lives of others.

Never forget that like you, your suppliers, your staff, your customers also have families they love, support and care for. We all share the same daily personal struggles of juggling children, aging parents, providing a roof over our heads for our loved ones and trying to hold our marriages and personal relationships together. Don't let the goal of having 'all the money in the world' change your values.

I want to remind our up-and-coming business warriors that there is much more to life than business. While we hear amazing success stories and strive to achieve these goals, I found the more successful we became, and the more money we made, the more time-poor I was.

I know what time and effort it takes to run and manage a rapidly growing company with twenty-eight staff. I can say in the last two years in my company was like going to battle every day. My yacht and sailing were my saving grace, my escape away from the weekly stress and chaos, and the real Safe Harbour in my life.

In the end, we are all different, and we need to embrace that fact in every aspect of our business and management. I believe it is imperative to look for people's strengths and know their weaknesses. More importantly, we need to unleash and encourage what people are good at. This way, it empowers people to feel good about themselves and not focus on the negative aspects.

None of us are perfect, and as my dear late aunt would always say, 'And isn't it wonderful how different we all are, otherwise the world would be so boring.'

LIFE LESSON: *Whether you wear five-hundred-dollar designer shoes or five-dollar shoes, they still fit the same feet and will take you on the same journey.*

Walking Away with a Smile on My Face

Now, after all the rise and fall of our beloved business, it is time to be with the person who needs me most in her final days - my mother. Over the past few years, her health had deteriorated, and I felt guilty that I couldn't spend more time with her.

Our Banaban Cause is still waiting for us. There is so much work to be done. It was the driving force behind my relationship with Ken. While the stress over the business nearly drove us apart, no one can ever destroy our shared love and passion for Our Cause.

Ken and I firmly believe the spirit and protection of our Banaban and Australian ancestors have always been there for us. We could not believe how blessed we were that the administrator could liquidate our company but failed to sell off our Banaban brand. The Banaban product name remains intact and upholds all that is important to us.

I know it may seem at odds with my story, but I cannot help but still smile and feel proud of what we achieved.

After the business closed, we took on a new mission by establishing our own publishing company - Banaban

Vision. We have been busy converting much of our extensive Banaban writings and research findings over the past thirty years into online and printed publications.

One of our main tasks was to upgrade and republish a second edition of the history of Banaba – *Te Rii ni Banaba: Backbone of Banaba*. It was wonderful for the two of us to get back to the history of our families that had brought us together in the first place.

We were not getting any younger. It made us realise how important it was to release our documents, printed material, photographs, artifacts, and other archives as a lasting legacy for the Banaban community. So, I came up with the idea to implement a closed Facebook group online, the "*Banaban Traditional Learning Centre*", exclusively for the young Banaban generation. It has been a great success.

Our rise and fall experience had another positive outcome. As I penned my last words to bring this journey to a close, I received a phone call.

The unknown voice on the other end of the phone stated, 'I have good news for you and Ken ... we have found him. We have found Teimanaia's skull!'

The man identified himself as an academic in charge of the committee for the repatriation of indigenous ancestral remains. His university had been advised of our mission and search of nearly thirty years. He confirmed that Teimanaia had been sitting in the university's museum section in Melbourne for almost ninety years.

It was a miracle—all the years of work, the dead ends, and an undying belief that Ken and I shared.

Our dream had finally come true.

How fascinating that Indigenous Australians were once again linked to our mission and Cause. The repatriation committee had paved the way through the United Nations and the Australian government for the return of indigenous remains. Through the protocols that were now in place, Teimanaia was found.

He would finally be coming home, and the Banabans given a formal apology from the university's museum. I cannot express how significant this is for the Banabans who have been denied recognition by all levels of the Australian government. They have never been acknowledged for the devastating price they paid that led to Australia's wealth as a farming nation.

Over the years, there have been times when Ken and I thought our Banaban mission was done, that it was finally time to walk away.

Yet, every time, there has been another email, another phone call and another request that we could not turn our backs on. Obviously, our ancestors had not finished with us yet.

While this is the end of our business journey, the work on our final legacy has only just begun.

FINAL THOUGHT: *Never give up, never stop believing. Your destiny and your future are all in your hands. It is up to you to make it happen ... Resilience!*

Now it's time to let you go...

POSTSCRIPT

The discovery of the skull of Ken's ancestor, Teimanaia, created great excitement, and we worked with the university's team on plans for repatriation back to the community. Simultaneously, Ken and I had adjusted to our new post-company business life, my work on this book was complete, and a launch date planned before Christmas.

But Ken and our ancestors had other plans. He was diagnosed with stage four lung cancer. Except for his worsening cough, he appeared fit and well. But this was far from the case. He was immediately admitted to hospital and began the fight of his life.

Within two months, his fight came to an end, and the life we shared was over.

I hope that sharing my words delivered at his memorial service will put this book, our business aspirations, family, and life values into perspective.

* * *

'My Champion, My Hero, My Warrior

From the moment we both stepped foot on your homeland Banaba, we knew our ancestors had brought us together 97 years later to right the wrongs of the past. How could the two of us from such different worlds give up everything we had known.

We spent every moment together exploring the homeland, during the day and under the magical power of the moon, combined with the spiritual connection of both our ancestors, it only drew us closer. Only our Banaban elders understood the importance of our shared passion for rehabilitating your devastated homeland and fighting for the Banaban Cause.

No one would ever realise the depth of feeling and commitment we shared. The need for justice and the importance of upholding Banaban identity from being lost so far away in a new land. A magnetic force within each of us.

The final test you gave me was the trip to your beloved sacred village site of Te Aka. It was so isolated and almost forgotten, surrounded by a sea of huge coral pinnacles. You made me show you the way, believing if your ancestors had chosen me, I would know the path. You smiled at me when I confidently pointed to the location in the distance. We climbed across the dangerous razor-sharp rocks, you, right behind me, ready to catch me every time I stumbled or started to fall, and sometimes you would clear the path ahead.

The commitment we both made that day stayed with us over the next 24 years through all the hard and good times together. The strong vice grip of your hands would be there for me for the rest of our lives together. Every time I faltered or was about to fall, your lightning-fast reflexes instinctively kicked in to protect our children and me always.

This was the real Ken, the man I knew and loved.

Yes, you had a beautiful smile, such a handsome face with a strong chiselled chin, but you were much more. For you, money, possessions and social standing was not part of your life. Your level of empathy, compassion and understanding of your fellow man was what made you truly special to me.

When you first came to Australia in 1997 to write our Banaban history book, we started a life together with no money, no possessions, yet we were so happy. I know how much you missed your family back home, and as soon as you were allowed to work, you never stopped doing everything in your power to provide for all of us. No job or wage was too menial in your eyes. Wherever you worked, everyone loved you. You would never let anyone put you down or demean your culture or Banaban identity. You never needed to prove your strength; it was so evident in everything you did.

While everyone saw the fun, smiling and eternally youthful Ken who loved to have a drink with your mates, I was so blessed to share my life with you. A life filled with tremendous and unbelievable adventures, challenges and ongoing debates that were truly special.

Our destiny had been predetermined to take us both on a journey together, one we never planned, but one we both understood we could never deny. Our family and close friends who lived and worked with us over the years may have only glimpsed this part of our lives, but only you and I truly understood how united and the depth of understanding we shared. Behind the scenes, we were a formidable team.

In 2004, our destiny once again was strengthened when your adopted brother asked us to market virgin coconut oil in Australia. How could we ever realise the importance of what this would bring us as you insisted that we should use the name – Banaban– as our brand here in Australia and worldwide.

Over the following 14 years, we would build an empire for our immediate and extended family here in Australia and Fiji and thousands of coconut farmers throughout Fiji, Vanuatu, Sri Lanka, and the Philippines. Every product carried the Banaban story to tell the world about the plight of the Banabans.

As our empire grew, we also had to face the hard decision of how to walk away. With so many outside influences as the company grew to a multi-million-dollar brand, things had changed. We decided that it was more important never to let the Banaban name be exploited or used to make millions of dollars on our Banaban story on the backs of your people.

You became so stressed over this. It was almost unbearable, so I took over the full responsibility of managing the company. Again, this was so foreign for you, Ken. You had always been an integral part of the company, my partner, my rock.

I knew where you had come from, your strength of character, yet at this level of our business, others thought you were a weak link—a way to get to me, to get what they wanted. And yet, through this very stressful period and angst, these opportunists never realised the depth and strength of what we shared.

We both decided to walk away with nothing and save the Banaban name and ensure our mission would never be exploited. This decision allowed you and I to return to life as a couple and back to where we started. Unshackled by worldly possessions and united by our Banaban Cause.

Over the last two years of your life, we were so happy to publish a new upgraded edition of our Banaban history book – *Te Rii ni Banaba, backbone of Banaba*. So far, we have already given away 700 free eBook copies to our Banaban community.

Only months before receiving the devastating news of your terminal illness, your greatest wish and pledge to your elders came true – the discovery and repatriation of your ancestor, Teimanaia. A quest that many of the young Banaban generation believed was just a myth. Over the years, you never faltered in your belief to find Teimanaia's stolen skull and make the young generation realise the importance of their true Banaban identity. While you faced disputes over clan rivalry, you always believed in educating your people about the strength their culture would provide them in the challenging years ahead. You turned what many believed a Myth into a Reality.

This was the Ken I loved.

You may have left me now here on earth, but you told me before your passing that your work for your people was complete. Now you will return home with your ancestor Teimanaia in the days ahead. I will be with you on your last and final journey.

Your name, RAOBEIA KEN SIGRAH, will now live on in history as a true Banaban warrior and proud descendant of his people, who gave your people THE GREATEST GIFT:

To hold your head high and be forever proud of being BANABAN. To ensure that Banaban identity is never lost but passed on for the generations now and in the future.'

'*My darling, I promise you will stay with me always. I can feel you leaning over me to kiss me goodnight. Even moments before you left me, you squeezed my hand to show me your never-ending strength.*

As you passed, I told you that your great grandmother Kaka Tina was waiting to greet you.

I pleaded with you not to leave me ...

I will always wait for you in my dreams, on the wind, as the sun rises at dawn, and as the moon rises on the night sky. Just like it did on Banaba when it embraced us both with its luminous glow.

Now it is time to let you go ...

I love you, my darling ... and I always will ...'

* * *

A great adventure had come to an end. Our family business promoting the virtue of virgin coconut oil alongside the history of the Banaban people had risen to great heights. But once our company had grown so large that we needed to bring investors on board to fund it, we paid the price and lost control of our company.

I hope I have provided valuable insights into successfully running a business and trying to avoid the many pitfalls. How to manage your time and space, recognise the genuine friends who become part of your journey, the importance of family and the personal tragedies that life throws our way.

This is my story, and how I did it my way!

ABOUT THE AUTHOR

Stacey King is an accomplished entrepreneur, corporate executive and philanthropist with extensive experience in highlighting and advocating for the Banaban people over many decades. She lives on the Gold Coast, Australia, where she shared her life with her Banaban partner, Ken Sigrah. They both believed their lives and destiny were intertwined.

Their family connections go back to 1900, with four generations of Stacey's family involved in the early mining industry on Ken's ancestral homeland. Ken's great grandfather was one of the innocent elders who unknowingly placed his mark on the document that would give the British empire the rights to mine their island for the next 999 years.

Stacey's brother is married to Ken's cousin, and the two families are finally united with a sixth-generation combining of Banaban and Australian bloodlines.

Stacey and Ken both shared the commitment to right the wrongs of the past and help the Banaban people. They never believed that their efforts to help the women back in the village would turn into a multi-million-dollar global brand. Her commercial interests are extensive, and she is still an active businesswoman in the natural health sector, operating an online company she has owned since 1998. Stacey is passionate about indigenous art throughout Australia and the Pacific.

From her first meeting with the Banabans in 1992, she worked extensively on aid projects to assist the Banaban communities on Rabi and Banaba Islands. She went on to become the founder of the Banaban Heritage Society in 1995. During this period, she was involved in the research and coordination of various Australian and international television documentaries, including:

Exiles in Paradise, 60 Minutes, 1993, Nine Network, Australia.
Banaba – Grief for an Island Home in the South Pacific, 1995, Foreign Correspondent, ABC, Australia.
Paradise Lost, 1997, NHK Network, Japan.
Coming Home to Banaba, 1997, BBC, United Kingdom.

Stacey has written various articles on the Banabans for worldwide publication over the past 30 years and presented papers on the Banabans at various international conferences.

Her other publications include:

Books:

Nakaa's Awakening, Land of Matang – Book 1 (four-book series), a historical novel based on the lives of Stacey's family, 2000, Banaban Vision Publications.
Te Rii ni Banaba – backbone of Banaba, 2001, Institute of Pacific Studies, University of South Pacific. 2nd ed. 2019, Banaban Vision Publications. A Banaban history written

from an indigenous perspective and endorsed by Banaban Clan elders.
Hunting the collectors - Chapter 17, The Banaba-Ocean Island chronicles, 2007, Cambridge University Press, UK.

Papers | Abstracts | Presentations:

Legacy of a Miner's Daughter, 2004.
The Cultural Identity of Banabans, 2004.
Australia-Banaba Relations; the price of shaping a nation, 2006.
The Banaba-Ocean Island chronicles: private collections, indigenous record-keeping, 2006.

Where to find Stacey King online:

Website: www.banabanvision.com
Facebook: Banabanvision
Blog: Banabanvision
Linkedin: stacey-king
Email: stacey@banaban.com
Banaban Official Website: www.banaban.com

To hear more on Stacey and Ken's story go to:

Banaba: The island Australia ate, ABC Radio National, Australia -podcast.
The Black Knight and the Iron Maiden, ABC Radio National, Australia story.

* * *

Today, with her children and grandchildren's support, Stacey will continue Ken's legacy and commitment to the Banaban Cause.

www.ingramcontent.com/pod-product-compliance
Lightning Source LLC
Chambersburg PA
CBHW050259010526
44107CB00055B/2094